CROW KILLER

The Saga of Liver-Eating Johnson

*   *

CROW KILLER

The Saga of
LIVER-EATING JOHNSON

Raymond W. Thorp
Robert Bunker

FOREWORD BY RICHARD M. DORSON

INDIANA UNIVERSITY PRESS
BLOOMINGTON

First Midland Book Edition 1983
Copyright © 1958, 1969 by Indiana University Press

Manufactured in the United States of America

Library of Congress Cataloging in Publication Data
Thorp, Raymond W.   1896-
    Crow Killer; the saga of Liver-Eating Johnson
    1. Johnston, John, 1822 (ca.)-1900.   I. Bunker,
Robert Manson, 1918-   joint author.
CT275.J689T45   923.973   58-8120
ISBN 0-253-11425-X
ISBN 0-253-20312-0 (pbk.)
10 11 12 13 14 87 86 85 84 83

Contents

Preface
Acknowledgments

frontispiece

LIVER-EATING JOHNSON AT RED LODGE, MONTANA,

ONE YEAR BEFORE HIS DEATH

FOREWORD by Richard M. Dorson

This spine-tingling and blood-curdling narrative should intrigue historians and folklorists for its method as much as it stirs the general reader for its drama. What we have here is the skeletal biography of a Rocky Mountain trapper and Indian fighter in the middle decades of the nineteenth century retold primarily on the basis of word-of-mouth sources. Oral history as practiced today by historical scholars is, first, an elite history, dealing with prominent figures deemed worthy of interview, and second, a record of the living. But many Americans whose experiences are worth preserving are neither famous nor alive. Their annals belong to what may be called folk history, or saga in the Icelandic sense of family and local chronicles maintained by spoken recitals and filled, like all enduring oral relations, with marvelous matter. The history of Liver-Eating Johnson has been kept going by this sort of saga.

We know that the mountain men, living by their woodcraft in the remotest reaches of continental United States, generated a vigorous oral lore. In their winter cabins and at their annual rendezvous, they ate fresh-killed meat, drank whiskey, and talked endlessly of their own and their fellows' exploits. Jim Bridger acquired the reputation of a fabulous liar for his imaginative tall tales about a petrified forest.[1] James P. Beckwourth found a sympathetic scribe who wrote up his *Life and Adventures* in 1856 in a work that Bernard DeVoto, its modern editor, has called neither history nor fiction but mythology.[2] Kit Carson and Buffalo Bill became the most written about mountain men, although in their cases the spoken tradition was swallowed up by oceans of print. Johnson knew and sneered at Buffalo Bill as a tenderfoot, and the worst shot in the West. By contrast, practically nothing has been written about John Johnson, the eater of Crow Indian livers. His legend begins with the scalping of his Flathead wife by Crows in 1847, his subsequent revenge, and the Crows' attempted retaliation in the following decades. These events occur after the first bold wave of mountain men who answered the advertisement in a Missouri newspaper of 1822 placed by William H. Ashley, a well-to-do army general, for "enterprising young men" to trap in the Rockies all winter. Not sharing in the glamor of the first generation of fur trappers, and indeed coming in toward the end of the Rocky Mountain fur trade, Johnson never attracted the attention of biographers, dime novelists, or promoters of Wild West shows.

But he did ignite the imagination of his fellow mountain men. The present script has evolved through four main stages: (1) the oral accounts of "Del" Gue, who trapped with the Liver-Eater in the 1850's and '60's; (2) the recollections of White-Eye Anderson, another mountain man, who at ninety, in the winter of 1940-41, relayed many tales, told him by "Del" Gue between 1885 and 1900, to his interviewer, Raymond W. Thorp, adding to "Del" Gue's hoard exploits that Anderson had heard directly from Johnson and from other mountain men about Johnson; (3) the researches, correspondence, and interviews collated by Thorp, a nonacademic historian of the fabled Far Western frontier; and finally (4) the dexterous literary splicing in 1957 of Thorp's data by the talented writer of the West, Robert Bunker.

Here then is the personal history of Liver-Eating Johnson from 1847 to his death in 1900, pieced from oral legend. We shall never know the full and exact facts in the saga of John Johnson, but we can be sure that the legend is honest, uncontaminated by hucksters and journalists, and conforming to the classic patterns of heroic tradition. Like other strong heroes, from Heracles to Tom Hickathrift, Johnson is matchless in physique, endurance, strength, and resolution. His fellow mountain men, Forty-Niners on their way to the gold fields, traders and soldiers in the Western forts, all talked of his immense frame and the power of his hands and feet, with which he could twist off a man's neck or kick him high in the air. True to the conventions of the Heroic Age, the Liver-Eater constantly engaged in single combat: with the twenty Crows who individually pursued him; with the treacherous Ute who betrayed his force to the Nez Perce; with Sam Grant the Negro cowboy; with the Assiniboine who had shot his friend Arkansas

Pete. Whenever he had his opponent at a disadvantage, the Liver-Eater granted him equal or even favoring terms, giving him first draw or tossing him a knife and then crushing him with a kick and a blow. Like Beowulf and Cu Chulainn, he grappled with monsters, and beat off a grizzly bear and a mountain lion in a cave with the frozen leg he had wrenched off a Blackfoot. His stamina is seen in his two-hundred-mile escape from the Blackfoot village back to his own cabin half-naked in a freezing snowstorm, a feat suggestive of another mountain man marvel, the return of Hugh Glass, mauled by a bear and left for dead by his companions in the wilderness, crawling hundreds of miles through Indian country to Fort Kiowa.[3]

True also to the epic formula, Johnson possessed prized weapons and a remarkable steed that share the luster of their owner. As with Beowulf's sword Hrunting and Davy Crockett's rifle Killdevil, the matching rosewood-handled Walker Colt and Bowie knife of Johnson became his trademarks. He took pains to regain them from his Blackfoot captor the Wolf, and when after the Civil War he changed weapons, to a richly encased stone tomahawk given him as a tribal antique, and a .45 Army Colt, these too became legendary. So with his horses, which recall the winged Sharatz of Prince Marko and Cu Chulainn's furious mount the Grey of Macha; Crow Killer's big black watched over his master, scented Indians, and allowed none but his master near him.

In keeping with the heroic character, John Johnson is a man of sentiment and honor, and for all his seeming savagery remains faithful to the code of the mountain man. It was the murder of his Flathead wife and unborn baby that led to his liver-eating vendetta against the Crows, and it was the Crows' respect for the grave of Crazy Woman, the maddened wife of an overlander befriended by Johnson, that induced him finally to make peace with his enemies. For all the hundreds of scalps he acquired, Johnson claimed that he never killed a white man. Assisting Portuguese Phillips on the last lap of his famous ride from beleaguered Fort Phil Kearny to Fort Laramie for reinforcements, the Liver-Eater gallantly turned back twenty miles from the end to allow "Portygee" the full credit. Loyalty to his fellow mountain men, and sympathy with the white overlanders, rather than a desire for wanton slaughter, caused Johnson to raid tribes who had taken white scalps—according to the tales. As an old but still active frontier marshal, he seizes two boys peering into a show hall from atop a barrel, bundles them under his greatcoat, and takes them in free.

A recurrent structure can be observed in the gory accounts of Johnson as Indian killer. There is, first, the attack by the braves on the lonely cabin and the killing and scalping of Johnson's wife or friends. Then comes the relentless pursuit by Johnson. The last scene portrays his destruction and mutilation of the booty-laden Indians. Even when the Liver-Eater lost his horses and mules to Blackfeet and had to abandon camp, he triumphed by his wits, leaving behind poisoned biscuits that his enemies consumed. Another facet of the Liver-Eater's legend, reminiscent of Daniel Boone and Leatherstocking, is his uncanny, almost occult woodcraft. He could unerringly sniff the presence of stalking redmen, identify a tribe from the ashes of their campfire, and himself stalk the foe unsuspected.

The present work sets forth what might be called the Heroic Age version of the Liver-Eater. According to Hector and Nora Chadwick in their great study *The Growth of Literature,* an Heroic Age emerges at a point between the nomadic and sedentary eras in the social history of a people.[4] This society is fluid, migratory, given to raids and forays, hunting and marksmanship, boasting and drinking, fighting and feuding. Above all this is an oral culture, antedating print, characterized by bards and reciters who relate the adventures of the mighty champions. In the United States the westering frontier approximates many of the conditions of Heroic Age society, and heroes of the Kentucky canebrake frontier like Davy Crockett, and of the fur-trapping Rocky Mountain frontier like Liver-Eating Johnson, show striking resemblances to the older heroes of epic, romance, and saga.[5] Far more than Crockett, John Johnson is a product of oral legend; in one instance Thorp and

Bunker trace five word-of-mouth transits of a given narrative (see below, page 84, note).

Two other versions of John Johnson that surely existed in the nation's unwritten lore would show him in a less flattering light. The tribal narrations of Crow, Blackfoot, Sioux, Flathead and other Western Indians, could they be recovered, would exalt their own braves and cast Johnson as a demon-possessed white ogre. Among the white emigrants, travelers, traders, speculators, soldiers, and gamblers who filled the West in the middle decades of the nineteenth century, the Liver-Eater often loomed as a pariah, a half-naked beast hurling obscenities at Missouri steamboat passengers as they gawked at the cannibal on shore beside his thirty-odd bleached Indian skulls.[6]

Whether John Johnson is to be thought admirable or bestial depends on one's own cultural outlook. To the mountain men, whose code and strengths he exemplified, he was a subject of laudatory winters' tales. These tales, with corroborative documents, form the basis for Thorp and Bunker's work, a work quite without parallel in American historical legend. The Liver-Eater takes his place with Greece's Achilles, Ireland's Cu Chulainn, the Serbs' Prince Marko, the Saxons' Beowulf, Grettir the Strong in Icelandic saga, Antar in Arabian romance, and other titans of the Heroic Age acclaimed in traditional song and story.

1. J. Cecil Alter, *James Bridger, Trapper, Frontiersman, Scout and Guide* (Columbus, Ohio, 1951), pp. 380-91, "The Evolution of Bridger's Stories"; Bernard DeVoto, *Mark Twain's America* (Boston, 1935), pp. 141-46; Stanley Vestal, *Jim Bridger, Mountain Man* (New York, 1946), pp. 206-19, "Tall Tales."

2. T. D. Bonner, *The Life and Adventures of James P. Beckwourth*, edited by Bernard DeVoto (New York, 1931), pp. xxvii, xxix.

3. The story of Hugh Glass and the grizzly is retold by Stanley Vestal, *Mountain Men* (Boston, 1937), pp. 46-61; cf. Alter, 25-35.

4. Hector M. and Nora K. Chadwick, *The Growth of Literature*, 3 vols. (Cambridge, England, 1932-40).

5. See Richard M. Dorson, "Davy Crockett and the Heroic Age," *Southern Folklore Quarterly*, VI (1942), 95-102.

6. Eric Thane, *High Border Country* (New York, 1942), p. 69.

Preface

ONLY a handful of the early-day Rocky Mountain trappers have been portrayed in print. Those who led the most adventurous lives, far from settlements, kept to themselves. A few imitators, like the self-styled "Buffalo Bill" Cody, became "great" only through the efforts of press agents. A number were masters of the tall tale. Some took to themselves the real adventures of others. The farthest thing from the minds of such men as Liver-Eating Johnson was the thought that they would ever grace a printed page. They did not set out into the wilderness to build empires for posterity but to hunt, trap, and trade.

If, however, a few of the Liver-Eater's companions boasted a bit for him, if we may suspect that a few of their stories are a mite taller than in first tellings, we can hardly wonder. A vanished day is hard enough to evoke, and the land where Johnson's day was lived is in itself a stage for the incredible. The mountains he trapped were higher and more foreboding than those which most others of his kind frequented. The winters he faced were colder and harsher, the topography he scanned rougher and more varied—and with far more opportunities for ambush. It comes to this: If vanity was expended by his friends, it was expended not upon themselves, but upon one whom they considered the greatest of his time and place.

East of the Mississippi, savagery, if not exactly tempered by the seasons' beauty, was at least not enhanced by the seasons' bleak rigors; and the reader may even sense some unexpected nostalgia when reading of massacres along the Mohawk and the Shenandoah. Song and story have spread an aura of hollyhocks around the name of Elizabeth Zane, and given to the history of Black Jack of the Juniata the gentle backdrop of laurel and sumac. But the lives and adventures of Rocky Mountain trappers and Indian fighters were seasoned only with the bareness of their surroundings, the inevitability of violent death, the horror of mutilation, and the stench of rotting flesh. DeHaas could hardly chronicle here. The Mountain Men's lives are to be told baldly—and one may suspect that storytellers among them sensed how that very baldness gave them their meaning.

The Mountain Men were fatalists. An arrow accounted for one, a grizzly for another. One was killed in an idle brawl; another froze to death, or starved beside his partner on the salt plains. A contemporary reports the outcome: One partner, the weaker, hands his knife to the other, saying (according to the survivor),

"Stick me between the ribs, ol' coon. It ain't no use fer both of us ter cash in. When ye gits back ter camp, tell Long John whar my carcass be."

Thus admonished, the "ol' coon" takes on new life as he stoically appraises his comrade's lean flanks. He does, presumably, wait until his comrade ceases breathing. Then he carves his steak.

Mountain Men, speaking or occasionally writing, achieved the same proper note of fatalism. Consider old Jacob Fowler's harrowing *Journal* entry concerning Lewis Dawson's death (despite the heroism of a dog), and sense, despite all his misspellings, Fowler's blunt accent, his Mountain Man's way of speech:

While Some Ware Hunting and others cooking, Some Picking grapes, a gun Was fyred off and the cry of a White Bare Was Raised. We Ware all armed in an Instant and Each man Run His own cors to look for the desperet anemel—the Brush in Which We camped contained from 10 to 20 acres Into which the Bare Head [bear had] Run for Shelter. . . . [The bear] lay close in the brush undiscovered till [Col. Glenn and Dawson] Ware With in a few feet of it—When it Sprung up and caught Lewis doson and Pulled Him down in an Instent, conl glanns gun missed fyer or He Wold Have Releved the man. But a large Slut Which belongs to the Party atacted the Bare With such fury that it left the man and persued Her a few steps, in Which time the man got up and Run a few steps, but was overtaken by the Bare. When the conl maid a second atempt to shoot His [gun] mised fyer again and the Slut as before—Releved the man Who Run as before, but was Son again in the grasp of the Bare Who Semed Intent on His distruction—the conl again Run close up and as before his gun Wold not go off the Slut makeing an other atact and Releveing the man—the conl now be come alarmed. . . .

"A tree standing in Rich," Glenn helped Dawson start climbing. But "the Bare caught him by one leg and drew backwards down the tree."

I was my Self down the crick below the brush and Heard the dredfull screems of the man in the clutches of the Bare—the yelping of the Slut and the Hallowing of the men to Run in Run in the man will be killed and noing the distance so grate that I cold not get there in time to save the man . . . It appears His Head Was in the Bares mouth at least twice . . . (His) Wounds Ware Sewed up as Well as could be done by men In our Situation, Having no Surgen nor Surgical Instruments—the man Still Retained His under Standing but Said I am killed, I Heard my Skull Brake—but We Ware Willing to beleve He was mistaken—as He Spoke cheerfully on the Subject till in the afternoon of the second day. . . .[1]

Such men had their pride. To shoot twice at the same Indian was not only a disgrace to the marksman but an insult to Jake Hawken, who made the best rifles in America. There are no marble tombs where these men died, no carvings—not even a pile of rocks. But for the tales of surviving comrades who remembered, we would know little of them today. The story of one, however—even the story of one notorious among them—may serve in a very real sense as the story of all.

[1] Jacob Fowler, Diary, excerpt printed in *Land of Sunshine* (Los Angeles, January, 1899), pp. 78, 79.

Acknowledgments

"DEL" GUE told much of this story. As Johnson's partner, Del shared many of his experiences. As good talker and good listener, Del heard and sorted out what many another Mountain Man had seen of Johnson. Some of Del's stories, clearly, came first from Indian narrators—Flatheads eager to tell what vengeance they had helped Johnson wreak upon the Crows, and Crows determined that their own proud action against him be known. And then, Del knew all this mountain country himself. He had the Mountain Man's precise memory for topography and for the step-by-step tactics any given terrain had inspired in whites and Indians battling for their lives: the study of such was both ruling intellectual interest and provision against one's own moments of hazard. Finally, Del had much of the story from Johnson himself. For even the taciturn Liver-Eater took to reminiscing in his later years, of a long winter's night; and he had all along been willing to fill in for Del such details of the action or his own strategy as Del could not see for himself.

Del told Johnson's story in special detail to "White-Eye"—J. F. Anderson. As one who had observed some of Johnson's exploits for himself, Anderson took special care that the story be set against exact physical background. He marked, too, Del's comings and goings and how Del had come to know of each episode. Over the years "White-Eye" took in more and more of Del's narrative and could specify later just when Del had first told him this—in 1885—or that—in 1900. And to Del's account and his own observations "White-Eye" added all he could learn from others of Johnson's old associates.

One of the present authors (R. W. T.) worked with White-Eye in the winter-spring 1940–41, to get White-Eye's own story. But in all White-Eye's manuscripts, there was no word of Johnson. Nor did White-Eye speak of Johnson until asked one day. Even then he spoke little, and in great fear; the interview was at once over.

Now the story of how young John *Johnston* became "Liver-Eating *Johnson*" has all along been widely enough known—but in various versions. He has been said to have earned his name on the Musselshell in 1873 or in 1876 or on another adventure in 1880; or on the Powder River in 1875; or in the Black Hills in 1873; or near Bismarck in 1877; or as late as 1882 in the Snowy (Big Snow) Mountains of Montana. As will be shown, all these dates are a quarter-century too late.[1] In most of the stories Johnson was known for eating the raw livers of Sioux. Actually, he never ate a Sioux liver—or anyway a whole one.[2]

R. W. T. had talked with enough old Mountain Men, over the years, to know that there was more to Johnson's story. The evasive answers he received to the questions he asked persuaded him only that those who knew the story hoped some time to write it themselves. Old Tom Renehan of Omaha did tell him a little of the true Johnson story in 1913; Tom had been a bull-whacker over the Bozeman Trail. And Smoky Mills, a Pony Express rider with experience all through the gold country, at least could set Johnson's dates straight: When Mills arrived in the West in 1865, he said, Liver-Eating Johnson had had that

---

[1] John X. Beidler's Journals, as published in Helen F. Sanders' *History of Montana* (Chicago: Lewis Publishing Co., 1913), are a particular source of misinformation. Beidler would have it that Johnson won his name as Liver-Eater in 1870, but Captain Grant Marsh met Beidler with the man already well known as Liver-Eating Johnson in 1869—see Joseph Mills Hanson's *The Conquest of the Missouri* (New York: Rinehart, 1946), pp. 116-119. Indeed, Beidler knew the Liver-Eater as such as early as 1862.

[2] But the story goes on. See, as a most recent example, the brief reference in Marshall Sprague's *The Tragedy at White River* (Boston: Little, Brown, 1957). Col. Dick Rutledge of Denver, talking with R.W.T. in 1932, stated, as White-Eye was to state, that Johnson ate only Crow livers, and that that fact was well known when he knew Johnson in the 1860's.

name for a generation; Mill's statement was backed up exactly by that of W. H. Jackson, who went into the mountains with the Hayden Expedition in the early 1870's.[3] Finally, Ed Johnson—*The Virginian* of Owen Wister's novel—stated the Liver-Eater's story in barest terms: "I knew Liver-Eating Johnson in the early 1880's on the Chugwater, a tributary of the Laramie river. He had a long red beard. His wife had been killed by the Indians."[4] But the details of the story still lay hidden.

White-Eye Anderson was almost ninety years old when R. W. T. asked him, in the course of conversation, whether he had ever known Liver-Eating Johnson. The old man trembled and turned gray. His wife, almost as old and dying of cancer, said at once, "I will have to put my husband to bed now, Mr. Thorp." She struggled to her feet and showed R. W. T. to the door. There she whispered, "He knows everything about Johnson, but he's afraid to tell." Johnson, had he by chance still been alive, would in that year have been almost 120.

But Mrs. Anderson wanted the story told. She had been a frontier schoolteacher, and there was still a wonderful strength and pride in her. There at the door she continued, "I have heard the stories a thousand times, but no one else." And when R. W. T. dug for those stories, she encouraged him: She had heard them now for sixty years, she said, since her husband was fresh from the scenes he described; and in those years she had never caught him out in even one small lie. She took to turning her husband's talk toward Johnson, herself; and though she had to stop those interviews when her husband was too tired to sit up longer, she would each time schedule the next interview by the door.

[3] Interviews with Smoky Mills before his death in 1925 and with Jackson (first photographer in the Rocky Mountains) in 1932.

[4] Ed Johnson had J. H. Reid write these words to R. W. T. from Calgary, Alberta, on July 23, 1940. After Ed Johnson's death in 1946, at the age of 87, Reid wrote R. W. T. in some detail about Ed and Wister.

The first stories came hard; most had to do with Johnson's later years. White-Eye was somehow afraid Johnson might still be alive and violent. But at last the material came gushing, for ten weeks. Everyone, white and red, had been afraid of Liver-Eating Johnson, said White-Eye. But Del Gue had been Johnson's friend and partner through most of their careers. Del had wanted Johnson's exploits known; and now White-Eye wanted to hand down this story of what the years of the Mountain Man had been like. Along with the Johnson story itself, he told of how Del had known that story, and of how Del had told him, and of how he himself had learned more.

More and more eager to tell what he knew about Johnson, and tell it straight, White-Eye took to thinking through each detail. One night, indeed, he took to worrying that perhaps he had given R. W. T. some wrong dates. Next morning he rose from his bed, brushed aside his wife's protests, boarded a series of streetcars, and crossed Los Angeles to see R. W. T. Finding only Mrs. Thorp at home, he stayed all day and finally left word that he badly wanted to see R. W. T.

R. W. T. took such notes as he needed for a nightly writing up of the stories told him, then checked what he had written as a springboard for the next day's talk. Such of the episodes in the following pages as Del Gue could have known of, are largely as White-Eye reported them; and that White-Eye spoke only what he was sure of, anyone who knew the old man could testify. There remained nevertheless the problem of checking—where?—and filling in. R. W. T. himself knew the country. He was in correspondence with men who knew Johnson in the 1870's and 1880's, but not in the 1890's. He knew the likelihood of many episodes, and he knew the way Mountain Men talked, from his own long association with the last of them. But he was long in piecing together a corroboration of what White-Eye had told—and the "corroboration," it must be admitted, is more by nature of a spot check.

Bureau of American Ethnology Reports were of course the

first and most useful check on White-Eye's general knowledge of tribes and terrain; they served more specifically as a check on White-Eye's complete accuracy and fullness, in the writing up of transcripts of the interviews.

George Reid, brother of J. H. Reid and the son of Bill Reid of Overland Stage fame, as one who had known Johnson personally, confirmed that "he received his name by killing Indians and eating their livers as revenge." [5] Pete Coyle, reached through White-Eye, specified similarly that he had "hunted and trapped with Johnson. He hated the Indians because they had killed his wife." [6] There was Doc W. F. Carver's testimony that in the 1860's Johnson was already a legend, often mentioned but rarely seen—and that the story of the "kittle of bones" was accepted as unquestionable by buffalo hunters and trappers.[7] There was confirmation of the identity of the Negro cowboy Sam Grant in Charley Siringo's *A Lone Star Cowboy:* Johnson could indeed have met (and killed) Grant just when Del Gue told White-Eye he did.[8] A number of old-timers had heard some of the Johnson stories through other sources than White-Eye (though presumably through sources deriving from Del Gue), notably George Ogden of Cooke City, Montana, who knew the story of the frozen Blackfoot leg.

One great break was the discovery of Charley Hall, an old cowman, who reported that he had known Johnson when Johnson was constable at Red Lodge in Carbon County, Montana, in the 1890's. The Carbon County Clerk obligingly reported Johnson's dates there, together with the names of men who had

[5] Letter to R. W. T. from High River, Alberta, dated March 7, 1949.

[6] As reported to R. W. T. by Anderson.

[7] Carver to R. W. T., during transcription of material finally used in Raymond W. Thorp, *Doc W. F. Carver: Spirit Gun of the West* (Glendale, Calif.: Arthur H. Clark, 1957).

[8] Charles A. Siringo, *A Lone Star Cowboy* (Santa Fe: Charles A. Siringo, 1919). In private correspondence, Siringo gave further confirmation by stating that Grant was killed "up north."

known him there when they were youngsters.[9] They in turn, and the pages of the Red Lodge *Picket,* led to R. W. T.'s discovery of Liver-Eating Johnson's grave. The Veterans Administration had known where he was all along—buried not ten miles from where in 1941 White-Eye Jack Anderson still so feared him.

There were of course false trails, like the report that Johnson had died in Calgary. There were stories which at very best could not be proved, like those about Johnson as a whaler or Johnson in the Navy during the War with Mexico. There were tales which simply would not turn up and perhaps were never told: perhaps Johnson himself had enough idea of storytelling not to give Del Gue the details of how he killed all twenty Crows assigned to trail him, singly. There are questions one would still like to ask White-Eye: Johnson must have had some trick in the way he kicked foes, quite apart from his strength and his quickness—else surely some foe could have dodged, then caught Johnson's leg; what then was the trick?

But White-Eye Jack Anderson is dead now, these eleven and more years.

The authors are deeply indebted to many other old frontiersmen for bits of information, and especially to Charley Siringo, to George Ogden, and to Andy of *Andy's Corner* at Red Lodge. They are further indebted to Dr. Floyd Shoemaker of the Missouri State Historical Society for some thirty years of help; to Mrs. Anne McDonnell, formerly of the Historical Society of Montana; and to the late Dr. Grace Hebard of the University of Wyoming. George J. McDonald, County Clerk and Recorder at Red Lodge, dug indefatigably for these pages, as did Frank M. Olson, Chief of Police at Livingston, Montana. Mr. F. J. Carey,

---

[9] "Pack-Saddle Ben" Greenough of Red Lodge—so named by the Liver-Eater himself, he reported—provided particular information about hunting and trapping with Johnson in the 1890's.

Domiciliary Officer of the Veterans Administration in Los Angeles, succeeded in locating Johnson's Civil War record.

Norwalk, California   R. W. T.
Las Vegas, New Mexico   R. B.
January, 1958

THORP'S LETTERS AND INTERVIEWS WITH MOUNTAIN MEN AND THEIR FRIENDS

Andy Anderson of Red Lodge, Montana: undated memo on Johnson forwarded through George J. McDonald.

Ed Barker: letter from Crown Point, New York, December 5, 1949.

Mrs. J. Da Lee: interviewed by Edgar McMechen, January, 1932.

Ben Greenough: letter from Red Lodge, Montana, November 6, 1949.

W. H. Jackson: interviewed by Thorp in Denver, April, 1932.

Ed Johnson: memo on Johnson, dated Calgary, Alberta, July 23, 1940.

Ralph Lumley: letter from Red Lodge, Montana, May 1, 1950.

Smoky Mills: letters in 1925 (destroyed in storage).

George J. McDonald: letters from Red Lodge, Montana, June 15 and August 26, 1949, and May 16, 1950.

Anne McDonnell: letters from Helena, Montana, June 13 and July 5, 1949 and April 24, 1950.

Frank M. Olson: letter from Livingston, Montana, September 5, 1949.

Charles F. B. Park: Statutory Declaration concerning Johnson, dated Calgary, Alberta, July 9, 1940.

G. O. Reid: letters from Radium Springs, British Columbia, March 3, 1941, and High River, Alberta, March 7, 1949.

J. H. Reid: letters from Calgary, Alberta, July 19, 1940 and June 1, 1942, and Cardston, Alberta, March 3, 1949.

Tom Renehan of Omaha: interviewed by Thorp in Council Bluffs, September, 1913.

Col. Dick Rutledge: interviewed by Thorp repeatedly in Denver, January, 1932.

S. D. Shackelford: undated memo on Johnson.

Charles A. Siringo: letters in 1925 (destroyed in storage) and letter from Tampa, Florida, February 16, 1927.

part one

The Young Trapper

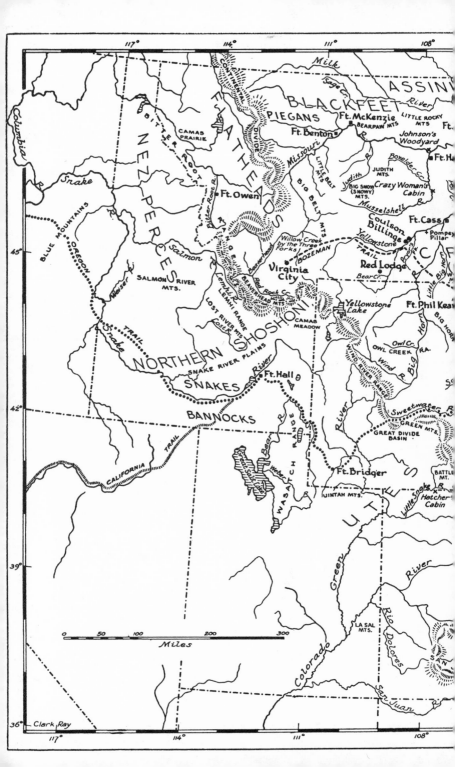

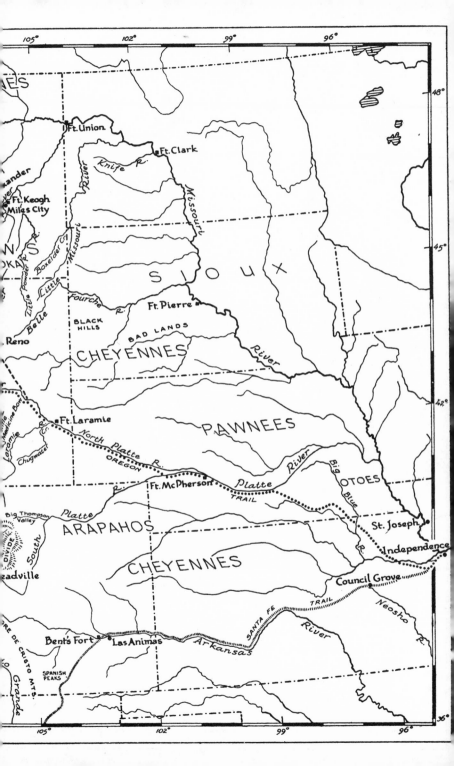

1 The Making of a Legend

ONE MAY morning in 1847, Crow Indians killed and scalped John Johnston's pregnant wife; for many years thereafter, he killed and scalped Crow Indians. Then he ate their livers, raw.

He ate them not for hunger's sake but upon principle—just what principle, his whole life's history may suggest. Other tribes than the Crows could arouse his anger; the Blackfeet indeed once shamed and mistreated him, their captive; but one tribe only did Johnston dreadfully humiliate. He was *Dapiek Absaroka*, the Killer of Crows.

As such he was feared; his fame served him almost as a weapon. Indians ambushing him, with every tactical advantage, broke and ran when he killed but one of them. As Crow Killer he might expect captivity and, therefore, the chance to escape when taken by other tribes, who would naturally hope to sell him dear to his special foes. On other occasions, as an awesome ally, Johnston could turn tribe against tribe and take for himself, in the warfare that followed, a highly profitable harvest of scalps. His first insane lust for revenge was surely real, whether provoked by the death of one he loved or by mere hurt to his pride; but the reputation it brought him was to become an extraordinary business asset. As John Johnston, the young trapper had already won a name for his strength and quick learning of wilderness ways.

Force and cunning, however, were mere details in his new repute as Liver-Eating Johnson: one whom the Indians could consider as obsessed, divinely mad. Johnston (Johnson) talked but little, and this added to his fearsome personality; he was known as surly, uncommunicative, mistrustful. Yet from the beginning he was willing to talk, when necessary, to set the record straight and inform his companions of things they could not see for themselves. He fell in first with Old John Hatcher, a famous but loquacious trapper who admired him and delighted to spread stories about him. In some of these first stories, Johnston was portrayed as simply the greenhorn: he had been cheated by that sly trader Joe Robidoux, and he had allowed Hatcher to steal upon him at his campfire, apparently unobserved. Yet, as the same stories went on, somehow the greenhorn had beat Robidoux in a horse trade, and had seen more quickly than Hatcher that a supposedly dead Indian was actually alive, ready to leap upon them.

Johnson chose as his long-time partner a trapper even more concerned with spreading his fame: "Del" Gue. Del, though as he put it he "knew when not to ask questions," did manage to obtain the answers necessary to the legend. Del went along with Johnson on his pilgrimages to the cabin of John Morgan's feared widow, Crazy Woman. Del witnessed the killing of the last of the twenty warriors whom the Crows dedicated especially to Johnson's destruction.

Del was not ashamed to relate his own queasiness when livers were plucked out and devoured. He also lived to tell his story even after Johnson's death of old age; in the middle 1880's and again in 1900, he told it to J. F. Anderson—"White-Eye."

The materials for legend were, surely, ready to hand. John Johnston's shrewdness and fantastic strength were of course the natural attributes of a Liver-Eating Johnson. Crazy Woman's shrill keening for her dead, each night come sundown, was as his Chorus of the Fates. His unfortunate enemies, the Crows, were tribesmen generally admired for their wisdom and dignity; and their very marking of twenty heroes to seek vengeance individually against one *dapiek* has in it their own sense of high drama. Johnston's associates, too, Mountain Men who when given the opportunity joined in his feuding, set off the Crow Killer's bloody history with their own eccentricities. As background against which the Liver-Eater's exploits might be savored and judged, there was the tradition of the private grudge. Should a trapper, beset already by unending work and harrowing danger, choose to run still further risk of bullet, tomahawk, or even the stake, certainly there was no one to deny him that privilege. Liver-Eating Johnson was not the first in frontier history to take a trail of vengeance against the Indians (though possibly the most spectacular). Black Jack of the Juniata and Lewis Wetzel won special renown for such vendettas, and there were others of the vengeful "Nick o' the Woods" type, too many by far to mention here.

Surely, as mere killer of Indians, mere bloody-bearded eater of red men's livers, the Crow Killer would be worth little investigation; we could easily dismiss him as inhuman or insane. But he was not simply inhuman or insane; he was not even simply cruel; he cannot be so easily understood. Rather, we may see him stepping back from the barbarities of others of his kind, almost as if they offended his sense of order. (They, in turn, at times seem more troubled by his choice of liver than by his mere cannibalism.) And though Johnson did express the generalized contempt of his era in regard to Indians, we shall observe repeatedly his very real respect for the warriors of many tribes. Even as in his heyday he was above all the Killer of Crows, a time did arrive in his terrible vendetta when—in sheer admiration of Crow magnanimity—he ceased his dreadful feuding and became their brother-in-arms.

2 The Hair Merchants

LATE IN the afternoon of a quiet autumn day in 1843 the steamer *Thames,* up from St. Louis, swung round into the famous landing eddy at St. Joseph. A blue haze, as of Indian summer, stretched from the far-off Rocky Mountains across the prairies to the Missouri, enveloping the trading post and the bright-leaved Blacksnake Hills. As the gangplank came down and the passengers walked ashore, the travelers found themselves under surveillance by the town's loungers, by beady-eyed Indian braves looking for who knows what, and by white riffraff hoping for some chance job worth the price of a drink.

One young passenger started up the dusty street, his belongings in a skin sack thrown over his shoulder. A brawny river tramp, heaving himself with a mighty effort out of the dirt, tried to seize the bag and was knocked down for his pains. With a roar of rage he was back on his feet, fists clenched. The young man swung his bag to the roadway, turned, and looked at the fellow.

"Don't ye like it?" he asked.

The lounger eyed his tormentor just long enough for a quick estimate. Whatever he saw, he did not like; he quailed. Wiping the blood and dirt from his face, he turned away. The young man went on up the street.[1]

If he spoke at all to his fellow passengers on the *Thames,* the young man must have heard of the old trader who had founded the town, Joe Robidoux. Joe was a wizened, squint-eyed, stooped and bent frontiersman who could cheat even such a shrewd competitor as Manuel Lisa; who would cheat even his own son. When, many years earlier, Lisa was setting out to trade with the Pawnees in rivalry with Robidoux, the latter asked him in for a drink, locked him in his famous whiskey cellar, and went on himself to trade with the Pawnees. And when Joe, Jr., fell heir to building lots in St. Louis worth some $90,000, his father locked him in the same cellar, this time empty of liquor, till

[1] White-Eye Anderson is authority for how widely what follows was told. Internal evidence suggests that Hatcher told the bulk of the story first, but Del Gue had from Johnston the account of his first reaching St. Joseph.

young Joe in his thirst traded a quit-claim deed to his land for a glass of whiskey.[2]

Old Joe was behind the counter of his supply store when the new arrival walked through the open door, swung his belongings to the dirt floor, and tendered a scrap of brown paper. There was no feeling reflected in the old man's face as he read the few sentences scribbled thereon. Nor did he show any reaction as he looked up into the face of the bearer.

What he saw was the powerful build of a six-footer, some 190 pounds in weight and yet apparently not full grown—a young fellow about twenty years of age. Extraordinarily long arms hung from his thick, broad shoulders. His hair was bright auburn, worn at half length; his face full and strong, with a stubble of red beard. One moment his eyes were a cold, light blue; the next, a dirty, flecked gray. Perhaps there was in them something remaining from his encounter with the brawler; Old Joe may have seen there what men would speak of later as their merciless depths.

"Ol' Hawken sent ye?" he asked.

"He said ye had three of his rifles to sell." Robidoux made no reply, and the newcomer glanced about at the goods displayed behind the counters. "An' I'll need some traps. An' a good hoss."

"Says hyar yer name is John Johnston," remarked the old trader, and the young man nodded. "Stay hyar the night. I'll fix ye up in the mornin'."

Johnston slept on grain bags filled with corn shucks on the bare floor of the store, locked in—lest he steal from the prince of knaves. It seemed to him that he had hardly stretched himself out before the old man had him by the shoulder, shaking him awake. After a breakfast of venison, corn pone, and strong black coffee, the bargaining began.

A Hawken rifle, brand new, of .30 caliber, cost Johnston fifty

[2] Rudolph Friederich Kurz, Journal, in Bulletin 115 of the Bureau of American Ethnology (Washington, 1937), pp. 66-67.

dollars. This was double the price charged at St. Louis—but not
out of reason. It was the best make, and meant all the difference between life and death. For his traps, however, Johnston
was later to learn that he had paid five times their value (since,
on these, Joe would not have to answer to Hawken). A Comanche pony, led into the feed yard by a Pawnee Indian, was
guaranteed by the trader to outrun anything bred north of
Texas—and cost fifty dollars more. An Oto tomahawk, surprisingly, was a gift. Johnston had brought along a Bowie knife,
purchased at St. Louis; so, equipped now, and stripped of money,
he asked the way to the best trapping country.

Solemnly, Robidoux tore off a twist of tobacco between his
snaggle teeth and turned to the Pawnee; after a few minutes'
palaver he spat and pointed west. "Thar's good trappin' out
yander on the Big Blue," he said; "this Injun will set ye on the
trail."

By mid-morning, mounted on the Comanche pony and with
his "possibles" packed behind his treeless Cheyenne saddle,
Johnston was on his way; old Joe, watching him leave, chuckled
as he pocketed his spoils.

Old John Hatcher was in Big Blue country by sheer accident.
He had set out from Independence with an enormous caravan
for Santa Fe—not in order to trade, not to help protect the one
hundred and seventy-five wagons (it was the largest caravan
that ever crossed the plains),[3] but simply to visit with old
cronies. At the Council Grove he left the train and set off due
north toward the Platte. As he approached the Big Blue, he saw
or somehow sensed human activity below the riverbank. A large
kingfisher, usually the most wary of birds, sat so low in the
branches of a small cottonwood and so engrossed by whatever
was going on down by the stream as not to see the approaching
horseman. Hatcher, with acumen developed in hundreds of tick-
lish situations, dead-reined his horse on the prairie, dismounted,

[3] See *Niles' National Register,* September 9, 1843.

and circled around on foot so as to surprise both the sentinel bird and the object of its interest.

To young Johnston, bending over beneath the bank as he prepared a trap-set, the voice of the Mountain Man came like a clap of thunder. "Cuss me fer a Kiowa, but yer back makes a good target fer a red nigger's arrer!" Johnston froze as—its fame as sentinel belied—the kingfisher emitted its raucous cry and sailed from the cottonwood.

A man may be a greenhorn but be possessed of intuition; and somehow the young trapper knew not to compromise his life by reaching out for his rifle. Instead, he turned slowly and faced his accoster. The latter stood above him at the edge of the prairie, holding his Hawken rifle loosely, but with the muzzle staring at Johnston and the hammer drawn.

In large outline against the afternoon sky, Johnston saw the very picture of a Mountain Man. Long blond hair hung well below Hatcher's shoulders; a heavy beard of the same hue graced his ruddy countenance. Over six feet in height and weighing well over two hundred pounds, he was dressed in the best cured buckskin from Blackfoot tanners, beaded and fringed with Crow finery. His moccasins were of Cheyenne make, and the beaded rim of his beaver cap was Shoshoni craftsmanship. From his belt of buffalo hide hung a hatchet, a Bowie knife, a powder horn, and a metal ring for holding scalps. Even as Johnston was taking all this in, the Mountain Man let down the hammer of his rifle and leaped the ten feet to the river shore. "What air ye a-doin' hyar, son?" he asked, and put forth a brawny hand.

Johnston led the older man's gaze to his trap, then explained, "I heerd in St. Joe trappin's good hereabouts."

Hatcher laughed loud and long. "That's a good 'un," he said. "This place war clean trapped out afore '25." He looked hard at Johnston—studied the greenhorn victim of Robidoux' practical joke—and saw in him, greenhorn or no, a likely partner. Kicking at the trap with disdain, he said: "Come along wi' me,

lad, but leave these things hyar. Whar we're a-goin' we makes
our own traps."

He next turned to Johnston's horse; he inspected the animal
very carefully, raising each foot in turn and watching the re-
flexes, looking at the teeth, and stepping back at last to watch
in admiration as the pony danced about. "Wonders come an'
wonders go," he said. "Now, how come it ol' Joe sold ye a
sound and fiery hoss sich as this?"

The two new partners ate boiled jerked venison that night.
They sat by a campfire in the vastness of the plains, and Hatcher,
ever willing to talk, spoke of Mountain Men and mountain
ways. Johnston listened and even asked a few questions; perhaps his native dourness was the less evident in the presence of
so much wisdom. When morning came and they rode into the
West, Hatcher pointed to his partner's present from Robidoux,
the Oto tomahawk.

"Don't use it less'n ye hafter," he said; and then, observing
Johnston's astonishment, added: "Spiles the scalp." Dressed
scalps, he averred, brought big money on the English market.

The young trapper wanted to know why.

"Hangs them up in their parlors, s'pect so," Hatcher sur-
mised.

They pressed hard for the mountains, since according to the
Mountain Man it was of the utmost importance that they arrive
in Uintah country before snows piled up on the Divide. They
made camp only when darkness fell upon the prairie, and were
up and breakfasted and on their way each day long before sun-
rise. When on the trail Hatcher was as silent and uncommunicative as an Indian. He kept his nose to the wind and his eyes
along the skyline. At night, however, when all had been snugged,
with the horses safely staked nearby, he spilled his wilderness
lore as from a flowing fountain. Johnston took it all in as they
lay quietly, feet to the fire and shoulders propped against their
Indian saddles.

"Allus remember, young un," Hatcher told him repeatedly, "ye must never give a red coon a chanst." Or again, "Allus be the fust ter count coup. Otherwise ye'll be nowhar!" Johnston was soon enough to prove that he could follow such good advice.[4]

For along in the middle of one afternoon, as they were entering the foothills, a dozen Arapahos swept down upon them. At first fire Johnston caught an arrow in the flesh of his right shoulder, but despite this he felled one of the attackers—while Hatcher downed two—before the others fled out of rifle range. The young trapper started forward for the coup but found himself peremptorily halted.

"We'll git that arrer out fust," said Hatcher; and with his Bowie knife he removed it, along with a quantity of flesh. Johnston stood stoically the while: "Now cuss me fer a Kiowa," said the Mountain Man, "haven't ye got no feelin's? Thet stun wuz deep!" Johnston's only reply was to load his rifle. ("Never come up on a dead Injun wi' an unloaded gun," Hatcher had taught him.) They advanced, leading their horses, toward the fallen Indians.

Hatcher took advantage of the occasion to expound upon Arapaho character: "These red coons," he said, "air treacherouser than most."

"One is still a-livin'," his partner told him.

For answer Hatcher drew his Bowie, and as Johnston pointed, the wounded brave attempted to draw his scalping knife. He was too late; the Mountain Man's blade was buried to the hilt in his chest.

"Now," said Hatcher, "let's git on."

He sank his Bowie into the soft earth and pulled it out again, clean and bright. Coolly he placed one moccasined foot on his victim's face, then reached down and twisted the scalplock around one hand, slowly, for Johnston to see. Now with the point of his knife he made a quick circle around the base of the

---

[4] Johnston himself told Del Gue of Hatcher's lessons; he was always eager to admit such debts.

topknot, and yanked upward. The scalp came off cleanly, with a snap like that of a whiplash. Whirling it round several times to clean it of excess gore, Hatcher deftly slipped the topknot through the ring at his belt, pulling it until the bloody side faced the sky.

"Dries quicker this way," he said, "now let's see ye try one."

As Johnston bent to his task, he was aware that the old trapper's frosty stare was boring into his back. But he was an apt pupil, and now he cut as clean and sure as his teacher. As he snapped the trophy, Hatcher spoke in some doubt:

"Never skelped a wil' Injun afore, lad?"

"Never seen one afore."

"Then cuss me fer a Kiowa! Ye air better built fer this work than any man I ever seed." The old trapper looked off toward the mountains and added: "Fust time I skinned a red coon I wuz cold an' shuk all over." He turned to peel the remaining scalp, then watched as Johnston mounted his horse and looped the topknot through the bridle.

"Slicin' a man don't bother me none," said Johnston; and Hatcher was to remark later on his partner's expressionless eyes.

Johnston did have enough—sentiment, can it be termed?—to save that first scalp of his own, stretched on a hoop, in his "war-bag." He identified it for White-Eye Anderson in 1871.[5]

If Hatcher taught Johnston how to kill Indians, he also taught him either the humanity or the profit of befriending at least some of them. He told, for example, a long and rambling tale of saving a Shoshoni chief's young son from a puma, which had already cut and slashed the boy from ear to chin. Johnston would, in later years, recall this incident.

---

[5] White-Eye commented, "Of all the hundreds of scalps he took, this was the only one that he kept with him."

3 An Apprenticeship

WHEN John Johnston went into the mountains with Old Hatcher, beaver had virtually disappeared and trappers had to take lesser animals. Hudson Bay agents and the despised "boughten Frenchies"—"mangeurs du lard"—encroached more and more upon the Mountain Men—trappers who prided themselves as white American freemen. Hatcher had specialized for years in the trapping of bear and mink, so he and Johnston went after these animals. Their years together shaped Johnston's whole career. Naturally, the latter devised his own skills (his surprise kicks) and developed his physical capacities (notably his sense of smell). Yet, even though he improved on what others taught him (for one thing, Hatcher's scalping technique), the fact remains that he was taught. His associates in his first years in the mountains, Hatcher, Bill Williams, "Bear Claw" Chris Lapp, and "Del" Gue, were remarkable men in their chosen field. The myth of Liver-Eating Johnson presents no hero sprung forth full-developed and ready for desperate adventures. Johnston's learning was remarkably apt; but he himself, in his own words, made clear the fact that he had had to learn.

From the first, of course, he was quick-witted and powerful; these were characteristic attributes. Trapping in the Bookcliff Mountain region of the Western Slope, he once saved Hatcher's life.[1]

Hatcher had wounded a grizzly; but the beast, charging from close quarters, allowed him no time for a second shot. Johnston fired at the bear but succeeded only in wounding and further infuriating the gigantic beast. His only recourse being the knife, he drew his Bowie and stepped between the bear and his partner, who was racing for the nearest tree; the grizzly, a huge male, at once faced its new antagonist, rearing up on its hind legs and

[1] Johnston himself told the following tale to White-Eye.

lashing out with its terrible forepaws. Ducking under a raking sweep of the claws, Johnston drove his blade into the heart of the beast. Then, as the animal swayed to and fro, he raced for Hatcher's tree—leaving his knife in the bear.

Hatcher credited Johnston with presence of mind. "Smart trick," said the old trapper as Johnston joined him in the tree, "leave the blade in an' the bar'll bleed inside."

Johnston might simply have ignored some general tribute to his strength or bravery or general field tactics, but he refused this credit. "Ther' wuzn't no time," he said dryly, "ter pull out the knife."

Hatcher's cabin, to which he took young Johnston on their first trip together, was in the Little Snake valley, on the right riverbank, in what is now northwestern Colorado. And to that cabin, with the help of Hatcher's two Cheyenne squaws, they carried their first catch of furs from the Uintahs. There Hatcher offered Johnston one of his women for the winter; and there he told his, and the valley's, history of war: how Henry Fraeb, "Old Frappe," died under Battle Mountain, pinned to a stump by a Cheyenne arrow, in a battle between trappers and an overwhelming number of Indians; how Hatcher himself had fought in the famous engagement of Battle Creek.

Johnston refused Hatcher's offer of the squaw. Indeed, in what he himself must have surely regarded as an excess of delicacy, he built himself separate accommodations, a leanto on the side of the cabin. Hatcher helped him build, then put the women in the leanto and brought Johnston into the cabin. The leanto, he insisted, was "good 'nuff fer Injuns."

Other trappers, passing through those mountains, came by way of the Little Snake to visit their old comrade Hatcher. Here Johnston met many shrewd and famous characters, men of long experience—and he was to observe how many of them died violently ere they could make another such visit. Visiting with an old friend was a pleasure worth weeks of hardship and deadly peril. But parting was casual, as even death amidst such everyday hazards was matter-of-fact.

Among the visitors was "Bear Claw" Chris Lapp, one of the best of the Mountain Men and a survivor of Sublette's band.[2] When Hatcher, as often, rode off on a one-man venture—this time to Bent's Fort on the Arkansas, with several packs of furs —Johnston trapped with Bear Claw. And despite Johnston's reputation for surliness, the two became good friends. Lapp could tell the younger man his own colorful history, but surely did not have to explain his nickname: Old Chris delighted in making necklaces of bear claws, and other hunters throughout the West saved such trophies for his collection. Using only the claws of grizzlies, sometimes as many as twenty-five sets to the ornament, he matched and polished like a craftsman handling purest gems. The claws from one of Johnston's first grizzlies being presented to Chris—by Hatcher—the mountain artisan proclaimed his thanks exactly as prophesied: "Great Jehosophat! Pocahontas and John Smith!" The hunter who drew Chris' most astonished praise for his offering felt rewarded indeed.

Bear Claw told Johnston mountain history on more than one occasion as they trapped together; later he narrated one exchange with the younger man as having occurred by Yellowstone's geysers. "Right thar is whar ol' Colter stood when he diskivered these bilin's," Chris said. Johnston, apparently, said nothing—whether in awe at the spectacle or because he had nothing to say. "Later on," continued Bear Claw, "Colter had ter run a hunderd miles from the Injuns."

"Why *had* ter?"

It was as much as Chris could do to persuade his young comrade that a man might sometimes do well to run from an enemy, even from the whole fighting force of a tribe.

On that same journey, Chris and Johnston found Bill Williams camped on the Sweetwater. That oldest and most storied

[2] White-Eye knew Bear Claw and had the following story directly from him.

of all the Mountain Men was headed for Fort Laramie and desired company. Bear Claw, however, had other plans, though he accepted with his usual exclamation two sets of grizzly claws that Old Bill had been saving for him. Williams was even more taciturn than Johnston, and as they went their separate ways Chris felt called upon to tell his companion of some of Bill's exploits himself.

In his first years of trapping, Johnston came to his full growth and, perhaps, strength. Even the most powerful among his contemporaries came to respect his six-feet-two, his 240 pounds of brawn, and what W. F. Skyhawk called his "pair of paws as big as a half-bushel of Montana wheat"; for in rough and tumble he could hold his own with any two of them. If, as Skyhawk said, "with one turn he could twist an Indian's neck off," [3] he naturally had to use extreme care when "huggin' " with friends. Del Gue has told that he once saw Johnston, in a trade argument, dash a Sioux brave to the ground with such force as to kill him instantly; in the resulting free-for-all, the young trapper apparently killed five warriors with his fists alone.[4]

Johnston contrived to use his feet, too, so swiftly and unexpectedly that no one seems ever to have found a defense. Throughout his life, he was able to set up each opponent for the kill by means of one powerful kick. Indians were demoralized by such tactics; perhaps their very fear and resentment of such an indignity made them less effective adversaries of the Killer who kicked. At the spring rendezvous on the Green in 1846, again with Del Gue as witness, Johnston's kicks enabled him to kill two Indians at one time.

Johnston had been appointed a member of the camp police by the council of assembled trappers and Indians. Since blood feuds ran riot among both groups, and also among the various

[3] W. F. Skyhawk in the *Pony Express* (September, 1950).
[4] Del Gue to White-Eye again, for both this exploit and the next.

tribes, the assignment was rough and deadly. At one time he came upon a Blackfoot and a Shoshoni, tribal enemies for ages past, knives in hand, each circling for the kill. Straightening out the antagonists with a pair of tremendous kicks, Johnston seized both by their necks and, before either could turn upon him, smashed their heads together. It was the opinion of the bystanders that Johnston had broken their necks in his powerful grip even before the double impact; both heads lolled sidewise as Blackfoot and Shoshoni tribal police carried the dead warriors away.

Under the tutelage of Hatcher, Lapp, and others among the kings of the wilderness, Johnston came to know the Rocky Mountains as well as the philologist knows the printed page. He was from the first inured to dangers and privations, and at once learned to detect the presence of an enemy. After watching him at work from time to time, such companions as he had spread word that he was the greatest man-trailer the Rockies had known; and he himself ascribed to his sense of smell, or scent, his ability to spy out ambush again and again. It was said of him that he could walk once around the cold ashes of an Indian campfire, then estimate closely the number of warriors who had been there and announce the tribe to which they belonged.

Some of Johnston's contemporaries felt that his suspicious nature caused him to be especially vigilant and hence never to be caught off guard. Others may have wondered: Did his apparent unconcern for his personal safety stem from his knowledge of each enemy's whereabouts and likely tactics? Or was he more perceptive simply because his senses were never corrupted by fear? He lived by gun and knife and his own brute strength. Self-preservation was for him, as for all Mountain Men, necessarily the first law of nature. Yet he seems to have consistently taken for granted his own ability to scent trouble brewing that might be greater than he could reckon with. He never attempted to dodge a difficult situation, yet he never sought an encounter or ignored one in his reckoning. His trade was trapping; the mountains were his home; and the killing of those who would disrupt either became, for one with his skills, merely routine.

But the vast number of Indians he killed? He would no doubt have explained that they were his self-proclaimed enemies and that they, not he, had begun their vendettas. Moreover, he would have added, he had more enemies than other Mountain Men because he never refused a challenge, never hesitated to enrage a whole tribe by dealing with whatever warrior attacked him.

But how would he reply to criticism of that special mark of indignity to his fallen foes—the eating of their livers, raw? Surely the eating of scores—nay, hundreds—of Crow livers was more than ample vengeance even for the murder of his Flathead wife. Surely Johnston's bloodied beard was the dripping mark of his abysmal inhumanity?

Perhaps the Liver Eater might have answered—had he found reason to answer at all—that his killing of Indians was never indiscriminate: that his whole life story pointed up his admiration of many Indian peoples, including the Crows; that he had more than once trusted his life to Indian sense of honor; and that, further, his instinct told him which Indians were friends and which were foes. During his lifetime, he might continue, it had been his only boast that he had never had to kill a white man (not even a Frenchman). And had he ever felt truly compelled to justify his own existence, he must surely have told how many men and women he had befriended: Crazy Woman, for instance, and for that matter her husband.

4 A Madness

IN HIS very earliest days as a trapper, John Johnston undertook a prosaic but profitable sideline. Five miles above the mouth of the Musselshell, in east central Montana, he set up a woodyard, where for many years (in times of lean trapping) he cut and dried and piled cordwood for the use of Missouri river steamboats. Here steamboats "wooded up," the captains depositing paper-money payment in a knothole in a cottonwood.[1]

And here, in the summer of 1846, Johnston returned with "Bigfoot" Davis from some highly profitable trading among the Flatheads. He had, incidentally, turned down a subchief's offer to sell him his daughter.

Johnston found some money in his tree-safe; and now the two separated, Bigfoot going down the Missouri to a trading post, and Johnston riding southward along the Musselshell. He was heading directly toward a wilderness tragedy.[2]

Having heard the call of the West, sold his Connecticut farm, and transported his family to Independence, Missouri, John Morgan, like other emigrants who traveled by wagon, put in his own supplies for the journey and then joined a train up the Oregon Trail. All went well for the Morgans until (as White-Eye recorded) the train reached a point near the present town of Beatrice, Nebraska; there Morgan quarreled with the train boss

[1] See Beidler's and Captain Marsh's corroboration, in Sanders, *History of Montana,* and Hanson, *The Conquest of the Missouri.*

[2] Although Del Gue clearly could have heard all the following from Johnston (and was indeed to tell the whole story to White-Eye), others besides Del were to join Johnston in helping Mrs. Morgan over the years and may have added some details Del did not get from Johnston directly. There is presumably no telling what Mountain Man first compared notes with those who had known the Morgans in the wagon train, and thus learned the start of the story.

and decided to go it alone. His start was near the Big Blue, not many miles from the point where Old Hatcher had taught Johnston his first lesson in caution. Stupid indeed was John Morgan to leave the protection afforded by a large train of prairie schooners with his wife, two small sons, and an eighteen-year-old daughter. But headstrong was many a man who left his Eastern farm for the dangers, rigors, and vicissitudes of a harsh wilderness.

From the Big Blue to the Musselshell is some seven hundred miles, northwest by west. In those seven hundred miles the Morgans and their oxen apparently suffered nothing worse than heat. When John Morgan thought best to stop a while to mend his wagon wheels—all the spokes had sprung in the heat, and a number had broken—his wife and the children were ready to enjoy the chance to rest. The wheels were mended in a couple of days, and the wagon backed into shallow water to let the spokes swell into place; but the Morgans decided to stay where they were for a week or perhaps even longer before proceeding. Morgan and the boys built a leanto. The mother and her daughter mended clothing in the shade. There was even time for fishing. Each morning Morgan turned the oxen out to graze; each evening he fetched them in close to the leanto.

On the third such evening, Morgan had not reappeared with the oxen in an hour's time; his wife, accordingly, sent the two boys after him. When they too did not return, Mrs. Morgan presumably supposed that they had simply not been able to find the oxen, for she sent her daughter also to look. But shortly after the daughter left, the mother heard her scream. Seizing an axe from the wagon bed, she too ran toward where she knew the oxen had been grazing. She was not long in finding what was there for her to see. A dozen Blackfoot warriors were there before her.

John Morgan was still alive, though apparently senseless and tied to a sycamore tree. The great blood-clotted gash in the top of his head showed that he had been scalped crudely with a tomahawk. Both boys lay dead; their scalps too had been taken. The daughter, in her last few moments of life, lay stripped of her clothing, screaming, held to the ground, raped.

Several of the warriors now ran toward Mrs. Morgan, but when she raised her axe they fled; perhaps they already saw, and like all other Indians dreaded, the madness in her. Berserk with grief and fury, she charged among them; and so inept were they in their terror that four of them fell under her axe. They tomahawked and scalped the Morgans' poor ravished daughter; they cut loose the half-dead Morgan and carried him to their ponies; they fled, so hurriedly indeed as to drop his scalp.

Young John Johnston, coming on the scene at the end of that August day, saw in a moment what had taken place before his arrival. Dismounting, he picketed the horse he rode and two pack animals heavy-laden with the gains of his trade in the Big Horns. He learned at once that he could get no sense out of Mrs. Morgan, that he was dealing with a crazy woman. He did help her to dig four graves and to bury her three dead; in the fourth she buried her husband's scalp. Johnston cut, sharpened, and drove four posts, one for each mound. He watched while Mrs. Morgan rammed down onto those posts the heads of the four Blackfeet she had killed.

Johnston stayed nearby for three days, long enough to build Mrs. Morgan a small cabin of cut logs. When he had carried her few belongings into it, along with some of his own supplies for her, he found that his stay was over. As he told Hatcher, next time they had both returned to the cabin on the Little Snake, "Thet squaw p'inted her musket at me. Pore critter, she hed me skeart." [3]

[3] Del Gue, who told this part of the story to White-Eye Anderson, may have had it from Hatcher. More likely, since Hatcher was already on his way out of Mountain Man country, Del had it from John Johnston himself.

It was a lonely winter for Johnston, on the Little Snake; Hatcher had pulled out for good. He broke his plans to his partner gradually: "Reckon I'll be gittin' on down torst Santy Fee," he said first, and later, "Mought even git out ter Californy; allus wanted ter go thar, an' lay my bones beside the sea."

Hatcher sent his women back to their people, the Cheyennes, with plenty of supplies for the trip and a pack horse loaded with gifts for themselves and for their families. He gave Johnston the cabin and its furnishings, admonished him "Watch yer topknot," and rode away to the southeast. Like the stoical Cheyenne women walking off with their pack horse, he looked back not once. Johnston, surveying his new properties, wondered why a Mountain Man should want to die in so alien a land as California, or be buried by the sea.

Johnston had plans already for the winter; he would trap in partnership with Del Gue, that Mountain Man of the twisting six-inch mustachios, who had been of Wyeth's company of New Englanders. But he remained by the Little Snake long enough to discover that the cabin had lost much of its charm for him. Though manager of a woodyard, he disliked cutting wood for himself. He hated to prepare his own meals. Actually, despite his dour nature, he missed both Hatcher and Hatcher's Cheyennes.

Visitors still came by, to be sure; from them Johnston learned that the story of Crazy Woman was already an epic of the West. Mrs. Morgan stayed by the cabin he had built for her, which is to say that she stayed by her four graves, refusing and even fighting all efforts to move her to the settlements. The buzzards picked the four skulls clean; the wind whitened them, and they glistened in the sun over the clean white snow. The visitors said that Crazy Woman hunted in the river brakes for sustenance. Mountain Men and overland parties helped her with gifts. John Johnston (as Liver-Eating Johnson), in particular, was to come by night, leave offerings by her door, and depart silently. Indians, and especially Blackfeet, kept far from that cabin.

Johnston learned, too, that Crazy Woman's husband had escaped from the Blackfeet—though just how he came by the information is a puzzle, since no one else seems to have shared his knowledge. Morgan never went near the Musselshell, never saw his wife; perhaps he too was crazy or had simply lost his memory. In any event, it was not Johnston's business to spread any word as to his survival. In the Mountain Man's code, a man's decisions and his silence about them were his own concern.[4]

5 Oath of Vengeance

DEL GUE KNEW, in the spring of 1847, that his partner had something on his mind. Partners often enough separated for the winter, then split their accumulated profits—simply in order to lessen the likelihood of a bad season for both; and it was agreed that the following winter Del would trap in the Big Snow Mountains while Johnston operated from his old headquarters in the Uintahs. But Johnston was proposing that they take separate trails now.

"Ye kin tek them furs inter Lar'mie, Del," he said of their huge catch of the winter just past. He did not elaborate, and Del made no issue. Perhaps he had heard Bigfoot Davis' story of the Flathead subchief who offered Johnston his daughter in trade. Surely he needed no assistance in selling furs, or in purchasing their year's supplies. So when the snow turned to water in the canyons, the partners packed their catch into small bundles and tied them on two pack horses; Del mounted and set out for the

[4] How the Mountain Men came to learn so much about the Morgans will appear in what follows.

trading post at the Fort. Johnston too packed a pair of horses with likely gifts' for an Indian, and set out for the Wind River range.

Early in May he arrived at the Flathead camp. Greeting friends he had made a year earlier, he accepted at once an invitation to the lodge of the subchief, Bear's Head. His well-loaded pack horses were statement enough of his intention; doubtless he announced, too, that in one winter's trapping he had become a man of property, with a cabin home, five good horses, rifles, and a number of Bowie knives.

First, however, the amenities must be observed; there were presents to be exchanged. The Flathead girl had not only a father but also a mother, sisters, brothers, aunts, and cousins; Johnston's packs were emptied fast. Bear's Head, having presided over the distribution of the presents (and setting aside his own), now heard formally, and appeared properly astonished, that Johnston wanted his daughter.[1] He repaired to his lodge for meditation, and Johnston attended a dog feast. At last Bear's Head reappeared for the bargaining. Three days being thus consumed, the price finally agreed upon was one rifle, two knives, and a supply of salt and sugar. (The presents already parceled out were worth five times as much.) Another full week's time having been given to the proper solemnities and festivities, Johnston said good-bye amid a roaring farewell salutation; he and his new wife then headed toward the northeast and the Musselshell.

The girl was known as The Swan, perhaps because her head had been allowed to grow with natural curve; through some oversight, her mother had neglected to fasten the usual flat rock to her skull. Possibly through Del Gue's description of her to his fellow Mountain Men, it is accepted that she was comely. Pre-

[1] Del Gue, as will be seen, knew The Swan and the terrains involved in the following story. But some of what Del told White-Eye may have come from the Flatheads through Mountain Man acquaintances; and Johnston's reconstruction of his tragedy, plus the account of his own actions, can have been first told only by Johnston himself.

sumably, since her father had put her up for sale outside of her own tribe, she was relieved to be the bride of a Mountain Man rather than of a "boughten Frenchy"; the Hudson's Bay men were reputedly brutal to their women and too mean to buy supplies of white man's flour.

To be sure, when they stopped to make camp on the trail Johnston sat idle and smoked his pipe, as was his right—allowing The Swan to erect a shelter, gather fuel, build the fire, cook, and break camp. But from the start The Swan had evidence that this man would not treat her according to brutal custom. He gave her a Tennessee rifle and taught her to shoot it; his bountiful supply of powder and ball was hers as well. Not too proud to learn from her—and although the sign language had served him well in the past—he set out systematically to learn the Flathead tongue. He was an apt pupil; they had no reason to hurry their long journey; they had time to know one another. They crossed the Owl Creeks and then the Big Horns; their trail split Crow territory through the center; they crossed the Yellowstone and headed for the Musselshell.

Upon their arrival at the camp they found Del Gue ahead of them; he twisted his great mustachios and greeted The Swan with no sign of surprise. He told Johnston that he had left the usual generous supplies at Crazy Woman's cabin. The two partners divided the proceeds of the past winter's work. Del left soon to trap in the Big Snows; he wanted to set up camp before the frosts. In two days Johnston and The Swan set out for the cabin on the Little Snake.

Johnston had only a few weeks at home, but in that period he could make certain of The Swan's comfort for the winter. At one end of the broad, flat shelf of rock in front of the cabin, he built a light corral for her pony and his two extra pack horses. He extended the clearing in back of the cabin to where still green brush, growing among a clump of aspens, now pleased the eye and a rocky incline sloped sharply down to the bank of the river.

The Swan baked white man's biscuits with white man's flour; and from dressed hides in the cabin she made moccasins for her husband in the style of her people. While she plied needle and sinews, Johnston pulled tons of grasses and lichens from among the rocks and by the stream, storing them in the small leanto as winter forage for the animals he was leaving behind. He was going, she knew, into the Uintahs for beaver and mink; he would return when the spring's rush of melting snows subsided. She could not have known, as yet, that she was pregnant.

The Swan carefully loaded his pack horses, and Johnston saddled his black two-year-old. (The two Utes who had ambushed him and killed his first pony, bought from Robidoux, had themselves died quickly; their dressed scalps hung in the cabin.) He mounted the black, took the lead reins in hand, and rode off down the valley. She stood and watched until he was out of sight, then turned and went into the cabin.

Through the long, cold winter The Swan many times rode out into the valley of the Little Snake, and with her rifle shot small game. Like all her people, she cooked and ate her simple meals outdoors; she sat cross-legged at times, staring down the river, on a rude bench attached to the wall of the cabin. She gathered driftwood, and when the big snows hemmed her in and the river froze solid, she was comfortable by her own fire. If she was homesick, she no doubt dreamed too of the geegaws and finery her husband would buy for her at the settlements when he went to trade. She survived the winter well, but long before the thaws came she knew she was with child; when the floodwaters spilled out over the valley, she knew that Johnston would soon return.

Perhaps she looked too anxiously for his coming. Perhaps she sat too long looking *downriver,* toward the bend in the trail where she had last seen him. The Crow warriors who surprised her came from *upriver,* from the mountains to the cabin's rear:

a score of young, untried braves on an expedition which was to bring years of grief upon their nation. Presumably, they rode single file, down the shelf of the flooded river's bank. They could not have seen the cabin from any great distance in that rough terrain. When they did see it, they likely split up, dismounted, and reconnoitered among the rocks.

The Swan, it seems sure, sat out of doors as the young Crows secreted their horses and applied war paint; for surely, had she come out only when the warriors were beside the cabin, her blood and her training would have made her more wary. They waited well-hidden until she arose from the bench and stepped for a moment into the cabin. In the moment's time she remained inside, more than one could have taken a deadly vantage point. When she reappeared, perhaps with unfinished moccasin and sinews in hand, they were ready.

Perhaps she saw the first freshly-painted face from the moment it appeared around the corner of the cabin; slow, pregnant, her work in hand, she could neither escape nor fight off warriors. Or perhaps she sensed Absaroka only as his tomahawk was raised above her; perhaps, her sensitive nostrils dilating, she barely started to rise. A war whoop rang out over the valley. The tomahawk thudded in the back of her neck. She fell sidewise off the bench. Her killer took her scalp.

The Crow warriors stripped Johnston's cabin bare except for a covered stool, thereby overlooking the large hinge-topped copper kettle inside. Apparently they counseled and decided not to burn the cabin, in the hope that, with luck, they might later surprise its owner. They took The Swan's pony and Johnston's sluggish, wintered pack horses, upon which they loaded their loot.

Johnston was articulate enough, later, about what had been on his mind as he headed for home, toward his bloody destiny. He had, he told Del, been formulating plans (in which, obviously, his wife would take part): he "hed been a-figgerin' all through the mountings on movin' up torst Laramie Fort, tekkin' it easy, doin' more huntin' an' trappin' an' mebbe a little tradin'."

He brought with him a beltful of scalps and an unexpectedly large catch of furs, his second now in two winters; even if Del's catch was slim, the partners' income would be greater than they had reckoned. Johnston had every reason to be thinking ahead toward a comfortable summer; but even as he "figgered" ahead on his way "torst" home, his gray eyes scanned warily the rocks about him.

When just below that bend in the river which cut off sight of his cabin, he drew rein. Dismounting, he took reins and halters and led his three animals behind the boulders at the side of the trail. In orderly concern for them, he stripped the loads from the pack horses and pulled the saddle from the black, making certain, of course, that all were securely tethered before he set out past that bend. Giant though he was, his long-striding double-moccasined feet made no sound. Threading his approach toward the grove of aspens at the edge of the clearing; slowing warily through the heavy brush in the aspens, sparse now and without leaves; dropping finally to his hands and knees for the last few yards, he came at last to where he could see his cabin.

He noted the dead silence; he felt the absence of life, in cabin or corral. Looking intently at the rock floor in front of the cabin, he saw bones. Cursing, with his Hawken full-cocked, Johnston stepped out into the open; moving closer, he heard a rustling behind the cabin and saw a huge vulture take wing.

The clean-picked skull of the Flathead girl lay near the open cabin door—wind-blown or vulture-worried a little apart from the remainder of her bones. Nearby, Johnston spotted a small round object about the size of an orange, all but disintegrated by the sharp claws of the birds of prey. "Two wuz kilt hyar," he muttered.

Dropping to his hands and knees, Johnston scanned the earth closely. After taking these first bearings, he strode to the back of the cabin and sighted upriver. The action being plain to him now, he took the trail: here, the slayers' horses had been hidden and here, their war paint applied. The Mountain Man grunted with a certain satisfaction as he picked up a long eagle feather. "Crow, or this child never et beaver tail," he breathed.

Still going briskly about his business, Johnston walked back and entered the cabin. As he had anticipated, the Indians had left only the stool—more a rude cupboard it was, boarded round from leg to leg. From it he took the large hinged kettle. Setting it down in the clearing outside, he elevated his head high, sniffing the air. Satisfied then that no Indians were in the vicinity, he gathered up the bones of his wife and his unborn child and placed them, with the single Crow feather, in his kettle. When he slipped from the clearing back into the aspens, he left no trail; save for the kettle from inside the cupboard (which his enemies had not seen) and the bones from the rocky earth (which could have been carried away by the vultures) all was as before his coming. Already the high mountains obscured the afternoon sun; darkness would come quickly to the Little Snake. He must hurry.

By the time Johnson reached the little pocket among the rocks where he had tethered his animals, dusk had arrived. Quickly he loaded his pack horses and saddled and bridled the black. When all was ready for his departure, he sought in the gray gloom among the rocks. Finding a deep recess, he set the kettle in it; then, very carefully (for all Mountain Men were skilled in the making of caches), he mortised it in with other stones of right size and texture until neither wolf nor bear could molest it.[2] At last he mounted, gathered up the tethers of the pack horses, and set out for Battle Mountain. He would make a high, dry camp that night, without a fire, hidden from any returning foe.

[2] Doc W. F. Carver told R.W.T. in the 1920's that the truth of the "kittle of bones" story went unchallenged among Mountain Men in the decades after the Civil War.

He was later to tell Del of that day's and that night's actions; but what moved in him as he rode up the slopes, he did not report. His secreting of the bones—and later visits to them—might be termed the actions of a man of sentiment; yet of ordinary sentiment, he was said to have none. Conceivably, he was merely protecting bones that were his.

At midnight, on the peak which had loomed over the death throes of Henry Fraeb at Battle Creek, John Johnston swore a merciless oath that he would be avenged—and mightily—upon the Crows.

part two

Liver-Eating Johnson

6 A Man's Reputation

It was in 1848 that the first news of Johnston's despoiling of the Crows spread through the West. Over vast territory where white men's campfires were few, far from the Absaroka's own lands and indeed wherever they hunted or traded, Crow warriors' bodies—and only Crow warriors' bodies—were found mutilated in special fashion: not merely scalped but cut beneath the ribs, and the livers removed. Del Gue, Bear Claw Chris, and Bigfoot Davis answered what questions were put to them: Johnston, they said, was eating these livers. What Johnston's motive was, they did not say; few knew even that Johnston had taken The Swan to wife, so short had been their time together. The general knowledge of Johnston's motives among the scattered inhabitants of that wilderness resulted only from an anonymous Indian's accidental spying out of a visit to his bones.

Naturally, the vendetta could not remain hidden. Within half a year Johnston became the Crow Killer (Dapiek Absaroka), or Liver-Eating Johnson. Forty-niners on their way to dig California gold heard the tales as they passed through mountain country and carried them to the coast. Mountain Men made an epic of the story. Many of them had, when hard enough put, eaten human flesh—but limbs, of course, never inner organs.

White mothers in far-flung outposts sent idling youngsters scurrying for cover with the admonition, "I'll get Liver-Eating Johnson after you with his knife." And when, at long intervals, the Crow Killer came in to such outlying posts as Fort Laramie, the womenfolk of soldiers and settlers closed their shutters and peered through the cracks at the dreaded *solitaire* who strode by with scalps dangling from his belt. They shuddered at sight of his great red beard, more crimson yet in their imaginations. They told one another that they had caught a glimpse of the cold, gray gleam in his eyes and that they had felt in his passing the chill

51

of Death. Proscribed, feared, and hated, yet respected by all, this was surely the loneliest figure this lonely West had ever known.

When Johnson did come to the post to trade, he brought Crow scalps and finery; and the furs he brought were of such quality that traders vied for their purchase. In return for these he received powder and ball a-plenty, so little flour or meal as to draw comment, and salt and sugar and coffee. The salt was subject matter for an eerie joke: "Do he salt them Injun livers?" But the joke was told at a safe distance. No one pretended in Johnson's presence to feel sore beneath the ribs (as was the common gesture, at mention of his name). All stood out of his path.

Johnson came in to Fort Laramie in 1851, the year, incidentally, in which Crow lands were bounded by Federal treaty, signed at that same Fort. (Boundaries meant nothing to him, of course, nor for that matter to the Absaroka.) Bear Claw Chris and Del Gue saw him there briefly, and Del reported his equipment. He still carried the Hawken he had bought from Robidoux, a weapon indeed by which he swore. From his belt hung a beautifully matched pair of weapons, a Colt Walker revolver and a fourteen-inch bladed Bowie knife, each with polished rosewood handle; report had it that these had been made for the famous Irish huntsman, Sir George Gore. His fringed buckskins, his moccasins, indeed all he wore was of Crow manufacture; all had been stripped from braves who had died by his rifle or his Bowie knife. As Del and Chris saw him then, he was the embodiment of Mountain Man pride and wily ferocity, without the Mountain Man delight in comradeship and conversation.

Bear Claw had not seen his friend Johnson for years; now he sought him out with a proposition for a trapping trip in the mountains. Johnson said tersely that he had other business, and strode away. Del pulled Chris back before he could follow. "Kain't ye tell?" he said. "He's on a trail!"

The Crow Killer strode to the feed lot where he had left his horse (and where the owner had regaled the curious with the traditional tales of that big black's exploits: how he could walk guard while his master slept; how he hated Indians and could scent them afar; how no man but his master could approach within kicking or biting distance of him). A crowd gathered to watch the powerful animal nuzzle the red-bearded giant, then stand docile as the Liver-Eater saddled him and tied on his purchases. Without a glance around, Johnson mounted, placed the Hawken across his saddle, and rode away, the black's nose pointed toward the west.

"Wonder whar he goes?"

"Whar'ever, ye kin bet ther's Crows, an' he knows it; he's on a death trail." [1]

There were indeed Crows where Johnson was heading; and he did know where they were, and he was on a death trail. Men had come to know that the Liver-Eater never rode without a purpose.

7 Twined Scalps

Now THE lands of the Crows, in mid-nineteenth century, were much as the fur trader LaRoque had reported them fifty years before. As described in the Fort Laramie Treaty of 1851, the boundaries ran thus:

Commencing at the mouth of Powder River, on the Yellowstone; thence up Powder River to its source; thence along the main range of the Black Hills and Wind River mountains to the head waters

[1] White-Eye specified that he heard this story at his mine in Arizona, in 1885, from Del Gue.

of the Yellowstone; thence down the Yellowstone to the mouth of Twenty-five Yard Creek; thence to the head waters of the Mussel-shell River; thence down the Musselshell to its mouth; thence to the head waters of Big Dry Creek; and thence to its mouth.

But Crows had ridden far from tribal lands to seek out and kill The Swan. The Crow Killer would pursue them, likewise, on these "their" lands or wherever they might ride.

Far away to the west, even beyond Fort Benton and the headwaters of the Missouri, there lay a country wild and primeval, its great mountains alive with wild game: the country of the Bitter Root Mountains. Here, each spring, came the Crows. This was Flathead country now; these fabled hunting grounds of many tribes, these green valleys and tortuous streams beneath looming peaks that had seen the wars of so many peoples, were not open to Crow hunters except as they came for war or on specified business.

The Crows possessed excellent qualities. They were proud, brave, and stalwart. They were not quarrelsome (like, for example, the Blackfeet, who were continually at war with this or that tribe). The Crow braves were good family men. Crow counsellors listened to the wisdom their women might have, though other tribesmen mocked them for such "weakness." The Crows were fine artisans and manufacturers, hence conventional traders rather than thieves and marauders. They were peaceful in that they did not seek wars; but when attacked they usually routed their attackers—taking more scalps than they lost.

The eastern third of their nation, to be sure—plains hunters who chased the buffalo—were subservient to a chief who lived more in company trading posts than among his people, and who was much given to drink and petty disorders. But the Crows west of the Divide, and notably their famed leader Big Robert, forever exemplified the nobility, the dignity, the wise counsel and fighting strength which had made their nation proud. It was the western Crows with whom Johnson carried on his feud.

Big Robert had sent fifty of his picked warriors to the Bitter Roots to trade with the Flatheads for horses. Their bulging packs held buffalo robes, necklaces of grizzly bear claws, finely beaded leather work, and eagle feathers; the Crows were the best tanners in the West. In exchange they would seek out the finest horses bred in the mountains, grown sleek in the green valleys. They rode as a cavalcade, with scouts ahead and trailing behind, and videttes spread out from the column.

Behind them, riding his big black horse, sitting in a Crow saddle, his eyes ever scanning the skyline and the rocks about him, came Liver-Eating Johnson. Somehow he had learned of their plans in advance; to trail such a column was mere child's play. There was of course no intention on his part of attacking fifty seasoned Crow warriors; even he acknowledged, later, that to have engaged in such open battle would have been "the foolishest thing this coon ever done." Rather, he bided his time until he could overtake them strategically, by night, at the forks of the Beaverhead.

Coming on the hot ashes of their campfire on the banks of that stream, the trapper dismounted, took four horsehide covers from his saddlebags, and drew them over the hoofs of his mount. Leaving the plain trail, he rode flanking it, slowly, carefully, silently, lest he alert some rear-guard scout. His sense of caution paid off, for shortly a Crow scout did pass on the trail, at a gallop.

When night came on, Johnson saw a flicker of campfires ahead of him, reflected against a canyon wall, where a tributary flowed into the Beaverhead. Picketing his horse, he climbed to the rimrock overlooking the stream and watched while the Crows prepared their evening meal. There he studied their camp arrangements, and made his plans.

Slipping back to his horse, Johnson quickly unsaddled, placed the animal on long tether, ate a portion of cold, jerked buffalo meat, and, crawling into a thicket about twenty yards from his horse, went to sleep with the animal as sentry. Two hours before daybreak he was up and about. Having made sure of his horse, he went back to his former vantage point on the rimrock. Below him he saw the sleeping camp. Two Crow sentries were on guard; one was dreamily tending the fitful fires while the other, in monotonous routine, paced a beat back and forth between the camp and the picketed horses. Highly trained animals, these were loosely held; some had already jerked their picket pins from the stony ground and had wandered a little apart. Near them Johnson saw a stack of buffalo robes and other trade goods, behind which he might hide in order to surprise the pacing sentry.

Slowly, bringing into play all his skill and experience, Johnson worked his way toward the horses. Once he felt that he had frightened them, and he stood silently for some minutes until he saw the culprit, an otter, slide into the water. Inching forward again, he finally reached the piled goods. From this base he meant to kill the sentry, scatter the horses, and thus put the half-hundred warriors afoot.

He considered. He dared not use his revolver, for he must pull the picket pins before awakening the camp. His Bowie, of course, was quick and noiseless, but the sentry might cry out before he could strike deep. Reaching down, choosing from the stones that lay at his feet, he hefted one that was as large as a young pumpkin and awaited the brave's return.

The warrior was larger than he had seemed from a distance; indeed he was huge, and no doubt powerful. He came within a few feet of Johnson's hiding place, glanced at the horses, and turned again toward the camp. He was barely four steps away when the Liver-Eater hurled the stone.

The missile was unromantic but effective. Caught just beneath his lone eagle feather, the Crow fell without a sound except the hiss of his escaping breath; the stone itself was noisier. Quickly Johnson seized the senseless Indian, lifting and carrying him to the scrub timber at the edge of the ravine. A few seconds later he was back in the midst of the horses, grunting softly to reassure them as he pulled the picket pins. Having freed them all, he scattered pebbles wide among them, at the same time whooping loudly.

As the dreaded yell of the Mountain Men rang out in the sheltered ravine, the camp of the Crows came instantly to life. Their own fierce yells and the shrill neighing of the stampeding herd mingled, rebounded against the canyon walls in the chill predawn, then were drowned out by the thundering hooves of horses in a dead run to the northward. Quickly the subchief shrilled his orders, and a dozen warriors set out after the maddened herd. Back in the scrub timber the Crow Killer threw the body of the huge sentry over his shoulder and slipped through the trees.

Some half-hour later, his horse saddled and ready for the trail, Johnson bent over the unconscious warrior. He seized the greased scalplock, ran the point of his Bowie around its base, placed his moccasined foot on the victim's head, and snapped off the scalp. Observing that a tremor ran through the brave's body, he swiftly swept his blade across his throat.

As he pulled a bull-hide belt from around the waist of the Crow, Johnson saw that a long-dried scalp dangled from it, a scalp with a wealth of long black hair. He imagined, for a moment, the ambushing of an emigrant wagon train, the crack of gunfire, the whoops of the Crows as they closed in after their victory, and the screams of the women. Perhaps this warrior had procured both scalp and belt together; surely his carrying of just the one memento, instead of hanging it in his tepee, marked its acquisition as notable.

But a second glance told Johnson that the trophy had not been torn from the head of a white woman. He ran his fingers through the coarse black tresses. As he looked closer, something familiar caught his experienced eye, and in that instant, in the clear light of dawn, the Liver-Eater knew certainly that in this, the beginning of his greatest effort against his enemies, he had met and killed the murderer of his wife. Quickly he braided the hair of the scalps together, the new with the old. Turning to his mount, he looped the topknots through the headstall of his bridle; and it was not until he had one foot in the stirrup that he remembered his identity and his oath.

Drawing his Bowie knife from its sheath, the Liver-Eater stooped quickly and made a deep incision beneath his slain foe's ribs. Inserting his hand, he felt for the liver, grasped it, and wrenched it free. Expertly he ran his thumb and forefinger along the blade of his knife and replaced it in its sheath. Blood dripped from his beard as he rode away to the northwest, skirting the ravine.

He had had a vengeance, he had killed The Swan's killer; but more than one Crow had had a hand in her death. Now, by having set a half-hundred Crows afoot, he had gained enough time to alert the Flatheads for their coming. The Flatheads would agree that one scalp might be avenged by any number. And they would welcome a share in such vengeance.

8 Crow Against Flathead

JOHNSON KNEW he had no time to lose; the Crows would be no more than a day or two in rounding up their horses, and he had delicate negotiations to complete with the Flatheads before their arrival. As was his custom on the trail, he slept little, traveling from long before sunup until long after sunset. He camped briefly—always on rising ground, where he could see afar. He knew, as he later said, that the Crows were never any more than one day behind him; no doubt scouts had surveyed the neighborhood after his departure, discovered the mutilated sentry, and so learned the identity of the killer.

After he had pushed his big black almost beyond endurance, he sighted the foothills of the Bitter Roots. The horse faltering within five miles of the Flathead encampment, and soon stumbling to its knees, Johnson sprang clear, drew his Walker Colt, and shot the suffering animal. He carried in his saddle, bridle, and roll, with some small help the last half-mile from Indian boys out lizard-hunting.

The Flathead camp lay secluded in a green valley large enough for the grazing of the five hundred horses the Indians hoped to trade, but small and secure enough for careful policing. Johnson walked through the only entrance, a narrow trail between two high and rocky knolls, after making himself known to the two sentries posted above him. Passing in, he strode on toward the lodges, laid out like a great arrow toward the path of the entrance. In the great natural pasture, fifty mounted warriors were cutting out of a vast herd the five hundred choice ponies, sorting them into bands of a dozen or less by color, fleetness, and training. Crows drove hard bargains—and knew horseflesh as well as Flatheads. Johnson wasted no time but made his way to the great lodge set off by itself, the lodge of Bear's Head, who had been a subchief but now ruled over his tribe. After a few words, the sentry pulled aside the bearskin over the entrance, stepped inside, then in a moment came out again and held back the flap. Johnson entered.

Bear's Head arose from a buffalo robe on which he had been reclining, and placed his right hand on the trapper's left breast. Johnson returned the gesture precisely. Such was Flathead ceremonial for a visiting relative; and the sentry could now report from his post the amazing news that a white man had come to visit his Indian father-in-law.

The chief clapped his hands for pipe, tobacco, and live coal; a woman brought them at once and disappeared as quickly.

(Among Sioux, Cheyenne, and Arapaho, a woman must have stayed long enough to light the pipe, but among the Flatheads she could judge for herself whether or not such continued presence was discreet.) Bear's Head filled the pipe, tamped the contents to his own satisfaction, and lighted it. Passing the pipe back and forth, the two men smoked for some five minutes in silence. At last Bear's Head knocked out the remainder of the tobacco on the dirt floor of the lodge. Now Johnson could broach his business; he spoke in the Flathead tongue. The old chief's eyes flickered, perhaps in surprise at the lingual accomplishment of his son-in-law. He took in his hands the trophies Johnson extended but at once discarded the fresher of the two. The other he cradled, deftly passing his fingers through the long black strands. The brittle skin crackled under his touch, and a tremor ran through his wrinkled hands.

"It is The Swan," he said.

The Crow Killer nodded.

"Many, many suns have passed?"

Johnson picked up a handful of sand from the floor and let it trickle through his fingers.

Bear's Head handed the scalp to his son-in-law and picked up the other. He had missed nothing, had noted that when Johnson entered his lodge the two had been twined together.

"They belong together?" he asked. Again Johnson nodded. The chief's eyes sparkled with hate; they held the question: Where are the others who came to kill my daughter? Where are this Crow's companions?"

"There were fifty; forty-nine come to trade tomorrow!" said the Crow Killer.

The old chief's voice came like the soughing of the wind in late autumn: "My warriors will be ready. We will trade death! We will count coup on these Crows." The two arose from the buffalo robe. *"Dah-pih-ehk Absaroka* they call you, my son," said Bear's Head; *"you* have already avenged my daughter; my warriors will do so for me." He clasped his own two hands together in the gesture of parting.

Two hours after he had held council with the chief, Johnson rode out of the valley, astride a long-limbed black three-year-old he himself had chosen from the picked herd, a sturdy, powerful brute well able to carry his great weight. Already Flathead scouts were out on the trail to report on the Crows' advance. At the narrow entry to the valley, two hundred seasoned warriors were making plans and preparations for ambush. With so many attending to this affair (though Johnson knew that two hundred Flatheads were no more than an even match against fifty Crows), he turned the horse's head southward, toward the Snake River Plains. He was going to visit his friend Wahni —"The Fox"—chief of the Northern Shoshoni.

Now the Northern or Wyoming Shoshoni were not mocked as "Diggers" like their lowly relatives the Fort Hall Shoshoni or the Lemhi or the Bannocks or some divisions of the Nez Perce, who subsisted on such little food—grasshoppers, even herbs, perhaps an occasional rabbit—as was to be had in the deserts and badlands and gorges south of the Bitter Root Mountains. But at this time these Northern Shoshoni were camped on Lost River, gathering *bia dumaya* (tobacco). The country through which Johnson rode was out of a nightmare, its streamways mere dry washes (except when cloudbursts came) or will-o'-the-wisp creeks, rolling along for a time on the surface of the rocky terrain, then disappearing to run underground.

The Crow Killer was in no hurry; and when camped on Red Rock Creek, he was overtaken by two Shoshoni braves on sweating horses. Learning that Johnson was headed for their own encampment, they decided to ride with him. They had recognized him at once; and he noted that each carried a Flathead scalp, recently taken. In daytime he contrived that they ride ahead of him, and at night he slept, as always, a little apart and with one eye open for trouble.

Thus they arrived at the encampment on Lost River. The dogs and children greeted the famed Killer with much bedlam. Older men, including The Fox, greeted him as a friend out of the past. Young warriors insisted they had at once known "the great white brave who kills the Crows and eats their livers." But all were puzzled to see their tribesmen along with him, alive yet carrying with them the scalps of his kinsmen.

Escorted to the lodge of The Fox by a warrior sporting four eagle feathers (for the four enemy scalps hanging in his tepee), Johnson entered. First ceremonials concluded, he went straight to the point. He spoke of the two braves who had accompanied him from Red Rock Creek.

"Each had a Flathead scalp," he said, "they fit along wi' the Crows, yer enemies the same as mine."

Wahni picked up a gourd rattle. The Flatheads were indeed his people's allies. And the great Crow Killer was his particular friend, to whom largesse was due.

At the first sound of the rattle the tent flap was cast aside, and a young man, a brave in his early twenties, stood before them. Johnson observed with special interest the long, livid scar that covered his left cheek from the ear to a point beneath the chin. "Yer son?" he asked, half in the affirmative, and the chief nodded. He gave the boy a guttural order, and he departed noiselessly. The two men now squatted, facing each other.

"Many, many moons past," said The Fox, "my son went beyond the Camas Prairie with a hunting party. He was but a child; chasing a rabbit, he became lost. A big cat sprang upon him from the rocks. As he struggled hopelessly, a rifle ball entered the heart of the beast. The shot was fired by Hatcher."

"I heerd thet story from Hatcher," said the Crow Killer.

"The Fox, as you know, is only a subchief," said Wahni; "Washakie has always determined penalties. But tomorrow when you go, you will carry the scalps of the two warriors who fought beside the Crows. I am sorry for their families."

When next he sat in Bear's Head's lodge, Johnson laid out before his kinsman two Flathead and two—more recent—Shoshoni scalps. The story was there to be read: two victims and two atonements; four gifts for a father-in-law; an opportunity, again, for the chief to show his people how their losses were ever avenged.

Hanging in the lodge Johnson saw thirty-six Crow scalps; only thirteen had escaped the trap at the narrow pass. Bales of Crow finery, too, were stored in a curtained-off space in the chief's lodge. All these scalps were Johnson's for the taking, and as much of the goods as he could transport on two powerful pack horses.

Two hundred Flathead warriors escorted Johnson with his cavalcade out of the valley. His black stallion was caparisoned with a rare white buffalo robe as a saddle blanket, upon which sat a richly beaded and intricately worked Crow saddle; the bridle too was beaded, and spangled with silver ornaments. Johnson himself was dressed in white doeskin, beautifully fringed and beaded and quilled, with handsome cap of beaver and new buckskin moccasins and leggings; and from his wide belt of buffalo calfskin hung, in bright scabbards, the rosewood-handled Colt Walker and Bowie knife.

The warriors too were dressed in recently gained spoils. They had feasted the Crow Killer, had loaded his packs for him. But despite such festivities there had been mourning in the camp; ambushed and outnumbered four to one, the Crows had upheld their storied fame as fighters. Sixty Flatheads had fallen.

Riding along the Little Snake toward his cabin, Liver-Eating Johnson may well have reminisced. Here was the bend in the trail where The Swan had last seen him. There was the glen where he had taught her the use of the Tennessee rifle. Above towered Battle Mountain, where he had sworn his oath of vengeance, now indeed fulfilled. Yonder was his own dooryard, where he had discovered her scattered bones.

That dooryard, that cabin, now had his full attention; he noted the smoke coming from the chimney. Bringing his Hawken to bear full upon the doorway, the hammer full-cocked, the Crow Killer charged forward, dropping the halters of his pack horses. Almost too late he saw a familiar jugheaded horse in his little corral.

A voice called: "Hol' up thar, pard, afore ye gits drilled." And then Del Gue stepped out of the cabin, his palms held outward in a gesture of peace. Sheepishly, Johnson let the hammer of his Hawken down as he dismounted.

"Thought at fust ye war a Crow chief," said Del, "wi' all them trappin's."

9 Winter Holiday, Spring Council

THIRTY-SIX scalps were like money in the bank—and Liver-Eating Johnson was a thrifty man, with no merely conventional vices. Once home, he doffed his new Crow whiteskin suit and put on old and greasy skins. He never drank. He would live simply and quietly this winter; though he gave Del two hundred pounds of coffee and sugar and salt and dried fish, his expenditures from his new capital came to no more than eleven scalps, spent at Bridger's trading post. He would give this winter to putting his house in order, literally. Del set off, with one of Johnson's pack horses as gift "to take the load off'n his jughead," for the cabin on the Musselshell.

Working only when the spirit moved him, Johnson soon transformed his single bare room into a comfortable haven. In a fortnight he had mudded up the chinks in the walls, hung buffalo robes about them, and spread three beautiful bear rugs—two black, one from a grizzly—on the earthen floor. He cut and dragged a huge supply of firewood from the river-bank. He thatched the walls and roof of the tattered corral and dragged in a supply of grasses from the valley floor, for his horses' bedding and food. Inside by the glowing fire, he had woman's work to do as well, the mending of his clothes.

The snows came late that winter, but when at last they threatened Johnson stood up one day from the rude stool by his fireplace. He took a beaded doeskin bag from its peg on the wall. Pulling the drawstring, he opened the bag and took into his hand a pair of scalps, their hair so plaited together as to be almost inseparable. Once more he examined that which was The Swan's, and that which was her killer's. Once more he fingered the killer's distinctive feather and his numerous body ornaments. At last the trapper opened his door and set out afoot, down the valley, for his cache among the rocks.

Long after he had climbed up to his kettle of bones, Johnson sat fingering two skulls: that which was a woman's, round though by tribal custom it should have been flat, and the other, far smaller and almost shapeless, of her unborn child.

Conceivably, Johnson knew that he was watched that day. Conceivably, that is to say, he had already sensed the presence of a lone Indian prowler who might report on the pair of skulls, the twined scalps, and the Crow feather—and thus make clear all through Mountain country that the Liver-Eater's coups were more than accidentally counted over Crows. Surely, it is difficult to imagine that even in such a moment Johnson so forgot himself and all his training as not to sense that there were eyes upon him.

In any event, the story would soon be abroad how for long minutes the fierce, red-bearded killer of the mountains sat fondling his keepsakes. At last Johnson filled his kettle, set it back into its crevice, and rebuilt around it his cache-like tomb. Before he looked up and around him once more, the black eyes watching vanished. And no bullet, no arrow came from behind rock or stump as the trapper strode back to his cabin.

Somehow, then, Indian eyes had been close enough to John Johnson to observe not only a large skull but a tiny one as well—and, of course, the Crow feather. There were Mountain Men who concluded, when the story reached them, that Johnson was simply "teched." But the lonely white women of trading posts and army camps thought the more of him for the story. In their eyes he was no longer a pariah but one who had nobly sought revenge for the murder of wife and unborn baby; henceforth they would allow their sons the privilege of talk with the great man of the mountains, should he come to trade. The Crows' Indian neighbors would laugh derisively now that a whole people could be preyed upon by one hunter. The Crows' fighting men, surely, would have to rouse themselves to reprisal. As if to ready himself for their campaigns against him, the Crow Killer slept. All around him, now at last, lay the deep snow.

He had awakened one morning from a heavy sleep and at once, as was his custom, opened the door to look out; the snow tumbled in on his floor. All the outdoors was a white blanketing over mountains, valley, and frozen river; and the snow still fell. With a rude wooden shovel, the trapper drove a tunnel from cabin to corral. His horses fed, he crawled back to the cabin, breakfasted, and turned to his weapons on the walls.

His Walker Colt he unloaded, disassembled, oiled carefully (with a vial of whale oil bought at Laramie), reassembled, loaded with fresh charges, and hung back on the wall. His Bowie knife, fingered most carefully and expertly, he whetted on smooth sandstone and honed on cured horsehide until the edge would part a floating hair. With the knife safely back in its sheath, he brought out bone needles and sinews and finely tanned buckskin strips, and set to making moccasins. One pair he fitted directly to his foot, but the next he measured to fit over the first. Kicking an adversary was more comfortable, he had discovered, when he wore two pairs—the inner set with the buffalo hair turned in.

Some said it was a Cheyenne, others a Blackfoot, and still others an Arapaho who had watched Liver-Eating Johnson by his kettle of bones. Somehow many tribes had taken credit for reporting this ludicrous joke upon the Crow. From the fierce and insolent Sioux to the wily Apache, far south, the story was repeated, improved, and magnified. At every trading post the Crows were derided. Did the Crows allow their women and even their girls to join in council, even to leap to their feet and argue fiercely? Then surely the Crows were womanish. Did they allow their children to romp through the council tent, upsetting their elders and creating general uproar? Then surely just such lack of discipline had left them vulnerable to their Killer.

Sioux and Blackfeet, in particular, mocked their ancient rivals. Fort Alexander, the Crows' trading post on the Yellowstone, was overrun by foes come to laugh at them. Sioux warriors stood in Crow fighting men's path to draw their fingers across their abdomens and cry, contemptuously, "Isantanka"—"Big Knife." Again and again the Crows took up the challenge, in hand-to-hand battle to the death; but in ever greater numbers they were beset by the laughing, sneering Sioux. Chippewas, bringing in their furs from the north, sympathized with the Crows but resolved to keep out of trouble. They hurried back on homeward trails, to repeat the tale of the long-knife warrior and his bloody vendetta.

Crow elders decried the wrong first done Johnson by young, thoughtless warriors; in their lust to count coups, they had not troubled themselves over what enmity their whole tribe might incur. But whatever the elders might think of original rights and wrongs, they must take action. Johnson himself had clearly forced the issue through his unwillingness to settle for any conventional revenge. And even should he call quits now, the

Crows must not let it be said that they had accepted such humiliation; to so brave and hardy a people, such opprobrium as theirs was insufferable.

Big Robert sat, stately in his buffalo-horn headdress, ready for council of war. He had called this council, to be sure, only at the request of his subchiefs; but if his younger warriors perhaps judged their chief by his apparent hesitancy, they had before them, strung across the front of his lodge, the signs of his plentiful coups, scalps both red and white. And if Big Robert had no longer quite the strength that was his when, armed only with a scalping knife, he had killed a mother grizzly —his impressive presence was still that of one of the greatest fighting chieftains of his time, one whose judgement no tribe imputed.

Stung, perhaps, by Sioux criticism, Big Robert had excluded from council chambers all but the most venerable of his people's women. He stationed stalwart warriors at the entrance with long strips of bark, tied with sinews, to discourage children and dogs. His own aged and wizened mother did hobble in. She sat now close by the medicine men as her son, in due time, called for opinions on how the Crows might best protect themselves from the Crow Killer. Warriors who knew the Liver-Eater talked of strategy. Big Robert's mother, in her turn, rose to say how surely even such an enemy could be destroyed, if only Crow fighting men would estimate him shrewdly. Finally Big Robert announced his decision. Dapiek Absaroka had already shown his skill in smelling out attack. Should twenty warriors be sent in a body against him, he would merely pick off those who might, in natural impatience and lust to kill, ride for a moment more rapidly or seek more thoroughly than the rest. In any event—Big Robert disliked even to speak of such a thing, but it must be faced—to send a whole body of fighting men against a single adversary could bring only further contempt on the Crows. Let the Crow Council, then, make use of the intrepidity of the very best of Crow warriors—their willingness to face death in heroic service of their people. Let the Crow Council consider how best to multiply the chance that one warrior, at least could reach the Crow Killer. Let a score of single warriors be sent on separate trails, to take their single chances, till one of them should prove shrewder or luckier than their prey. Let none of the braves return till the white killer was dead.

Big Robert's mother it was who went among the braves selecting, from among the fiercest and most agile, this one for his rashness and that for his cunning, another for his lightning speed and yet another for endurance. Her black eyes snapping, she whispered to each she chose their people's demand that they give themselves unreservedly. Indeed, though some of those chosen sought their foe for years, they were none of them to return.

10 . . . A Missing Chapter

FORTUNATELY, perhaps, John Johnson never told how he destroyed twenty such Crow warriors, one by one; and since during the years when he killed the first seventeen of them he still kept himself pretty much alone, fellow Mountain Men observed his killing of only two.

No doubt the story of all twenty killings would illustrate the full extent of Johnson's craft and above all his capacity for estimating others' craft, his readiness for his opponents' every variety of move. But in any such story the refrain—"He snapped off the scalp, he carved under the ribs, he ate the dripping liver"—must become not merely monotonous but intolerably sickening. Liver-Eating Johnson likely served his saga best by leaving this chapter to his contemporaries', and our, imaginations.

Only one fact did he provide: that each of the twenty was slain hand to hand. Each, in his last moments, knew himself victim of the Crow Killer.

part three

A Man Among Men

Crow Indian Chief and his staff, of the late 1890's

Crow Indians taking a tribal oath

A Crow warrior waiting for the signal

11 The Eighteenth Warrior

FROM ALL accounts, Liver-Eating Johnson was astonished by the respect and above all the desire for friendship suddenly shown him throughout mountain country. But apparently the warmth of feeling expressed by some of those with whom he came in contact was not displeasing to him. At length, like any gregarious Mountain Man, he took to visiting the camps of other trappers from time to time, and swapping news about trade and the tribes. His own story he saved, though, for a very few old comrades, especially old Bear Claw Lapp, Bigfoot Davis, and of course Del Gue. Even now Del asked Johnson no more questions than Johnson apparently wanted to answer; but the details Del observed for himself are enough to give the impression of a Johnson almost comfortably settled into his "family"—the few close friends—and his "place"—a thousand miles of wilderness. This is a Johnson who seeks no trouble with any man, not even with Crows, and who is really rather appalled when Mountain Men outside his immediate "family" come bursting around to stage him a "revenge" against some Blackfeet.

One's vengeance, by Johnson's code, should be one's own. What one could do for a friend was outfit him anew in his time of need, accept his ministrations in one's own time of sickness, and perhaps (as with Portuguese Phillips) help him through some desperate adventure, then pull out so that glory might be his alone.

By prearrangement, Johnson met Del Gue at Fort Pierre in the spring of 1855. Typically, this first re-entry into partnership was for Johnson primarily an act of friendship; for Del the year before had been captured by the Sioux and, barely escaping with his scalp, had lost his pack of furs. Traveling with Johnson to the Wind River Mountains, he could figure to recover himself financially. Johnson purchased the necessary outfit for both, and they were off.

The camp on the Musselshell was conveniently on the way, and accordingly Johnson could pass by Crazy Woman's place. Nine years now after her tragedy, Jane Morgan had many assistants among the Mountain Men; yet Del was a little surprised to gather how regularly Johnson had checked in through the years of his feuding with the Crows. And after Johnson, afoot for the last hundred yards, had carried in provisions, Del was fair startled. They were mounted again and riding behind the cabin to get back on the river trail when suddenly Del drew rein. "Somethin' peculyar hyar!" he cried.

They faced the quadrangle of graves with the four posts at the corners, a grinning skull on each. Johnson too pulled up, to hear whatever his partner had to say.

"Them skulls," Del said. "They're shiny, they're new."

Johnson chuckled. "Sure, skulls don't last," he said. "We puts new ones up reg'lar."

Del, by his own story, asked who "we" might be, besides Johnson himself. And when Johnson suggested that maybe Old John Hatcher might have come back—that there was some story of how he hadn't gone to California after all but was "a-trappin' way down on ther Colorady"—Del was for once ready to ask even more questions. He got nowhere.

"Come on, it's a-gettin' late," Johnson said. "Ye know what that means!"

Del did know how Crazy Woman took the coming of darkness, that hour at which she had been bereaved. Indeed the trappers were hardly a quarter-mile distant from the cabin when they heard her piercing shrieks. "If'n ther Blackfoots heerd thet, they'd drop dead!" said Del.

After two nights in their own camp on the Musselshell, the partners started on their long trail, south to the Wind River Range. At a trappers' camp on the Big Horn they found Bear

Claw nursing critical wounds but lively enough to make a good story of how he had earned them, in a scrap with a grizzly not dead, as it had seemed, but merely stunned by a bullet.

"B'ar git ye?" Johnson asked.

"Great Jehosophat, Pocahontas and John Smith, no!" the old man roared, and he shook the bear's huge claws in Johnson's face. "Ye stay the night now, I kin take care of ye," he insisted; and despite his guests' protests that he was still weak they had to accept his hospitality. "No liver," he said as in apology, "jist fresh ven'son."

The partners would be eight days riding after they left Bear Claw. On the seventh, Del was concerned to find the ashes of an Indian campfire where none was to be expected; but Johnson assured him that those who had camped there were Blackfeet. They rode on steadily and that night made camp on Owl Creek, in an old cabin Johnson had used many times before.

Del kept a close watch to see whether his partner's apparent unconcern was real. As darkness came on, their campfire crackled and glowed in the darkness, lighting up the fringes of the brushy copse among the rocks around them but making of the trappers themselves all too obvious a target for a foe.

Finally Del could restrain himself no longer. "Ye said them last ashes war Blackfoot. Kain't ye tell Blackfoots from Crows no more?"

Johnson grinned, knocked out his pipe, and slowly rose from the log where he sat. "Figgered mebbe I could make ye think ye didn't know," he said, "but reckon ye did. Kick out thet fire, Del." He stepped lightly back into the scrub. Del did quickly scatter the embers and stamp them out. Then he too stepped away, into the shadows with his rifle full-cocked.

For several minutes Del stood straining to hear some sound of what might be going on, but all that came to him was the sound of the munching horses, tethered nearby. At last he heard a muffled obscenity—Johnson's, he thought—and a grunt in another voice. There was, mixed in with these sounds, the thud of moccasin brought heavily against flesh. Into the faint light still shed by a few smoldering embers there sailed, his rear quarters highest, a huge Crow warrior.

The warrior had no sooner scrambled to his feet than he found himself facing Johnson, come after him with extraordinary speed. He had time only to lift his tomahawk; before he could bring it down, another mighty kick from Johnson caught him in the groin, and the weapon fell from his hand. Johnson stepped in and, with what now seemed slow deliberation, buried his Bowie in the Crow's chest; in fact, the entire action had taken only a few seconds. "Let's hev us a fire ag'in, Del," the Crow Killer said.

Del did rebuild the fire, though remonstrating that there might be other Indians in the vicinity. Johnson sat on his log again and filled and lit his pipe. "This'n," he said "air number eighteen. Jist two of their twenty left."

This was an occasion, if there was ever to be one, for inquiry into Johnson's feuding. Indeed Del secured that night an almost academic analysis of methods. First, there was the strategy of the kick to be explained. Johnson "kicked them into position," he said; hadn't Del noticed how "nat'rally" the brave, trying to straighten up after the kick, had instead "ended up" on Johnson's "sticker"?

After a few moments of smoking and meditating, Johnson stood up again, tested the edge of his knife on his thumb, and began another sort of demonstration for Del. He grasped the dead man by his topknot, ran the point of the blade in the familiar pattern around its base, then whipped off the scalp in so dexterous a movement that, Del swore, the head could not be seen to move. By way of commentary, Johnson pointed out that he had not—as was conventional and as Hatcher had long ago taught him—placed his foot on the victim's head. He had discarded this technique long ago as an unnecessary reliance on strength rather than precision. Hatcher, of course, could be excused for not having achieved such refinement of method: "Thet coon never had no practice like I did!"

The Crow Killer leaned once more over his victim, and his partner, well aware of the next step in his practice, endeavored to postpone that bloody moment. "How many reds ye reckon ye've skelped?"

"Wagh," the casual answer came, "oh, mebbe, not countin' a few pore Diggers, some four, five hundred." He threw the scalp to his partner and stooped again, knife still in hand.

"Don't, Liver-Eatin'; don't do thet! Now, Liver-Eatin', I'm a-goin' ter gag."

"Gag, then," Johnson said, and with a delicate sweep of his Bowie he opened the dead Crow's abdomen. Then he thrust his hand inside.

12 Captive of the Blackfeet

In the early fall of 1861, the Crow Killer helped Del set up a winter trapping camp east of the Continental Divide, in the rough country toward the North Platte in Wyoming. As in their other years of partnership, their plan was to pool the profits of separate adventures. Del was in a trapping location Bigfoot Davis had recommended, and would use Bigfoot's leanto for shelter. Johnson helped Del set out his trap lines, then set out to trade in the camp of his Flathead kin, in the Bitter Root Mountains.

Now it must be stated at once that, by his own standards, Johnson deserved some of the punishment he was to take on that expedition. The product he planned to offer the Flatheads, in trade, was one he would not touch himself. He had purchased two twenty-gallon kegs of whiskey from a trader on the Mis-

souri. The sale of whiskey to Indians, granted, was not as direct
an incitement to murder as the sale of rifles (which, of course,
Johnson damned as violently as any other Mountain Man). But
—though some Indians even then could drink companionably—
as yet most had learned nothing about alcohol but the frenzy a
keg could add when already excited warriors drank together.
Ironically, Johnson was to see his whiskey drunk by despised
Blackfeet, as their prisoner.

Del Gue had one protest to make, that no horse could carry
such a load as forty gallons (and likely Johnson did move more
slowly and more noisily than usual on that trip). But Johnson
laughed. Besides a pair of pack horses to carry his usual trading items, he had a powerful sorrel stallion; and in a specially
prepared heavy canvas sling, the kegs rode easily. On his own
big black, the Liver-Eater mixed his good-byes to Del with some
derision for his lack of faith in a "mounting hoss." And he set
out on his five-hundred-mile journey west.

Once alone on the trail, Johnson was his watchful self. He
moved his animals slowly, for he knew the dangers ahead of
him; and the loss of so much whiskey would in itself be as the
loss of a good season's catch of furs. He knew he must watch
not only for Crow warriors but especially for Blackfeet, now on
the warpath. His route was to take him across the Sweetwater,
through the headwaters of the Green Mountains, and into the
hazardous Owl Creek range. Whole wagon trains of emigrants
had been massacred there, and more trappers had died in that
stretch of Indian country than in any other. Johnson drew on all
his remarkable powers of observation and instinct to protect his
life and cargo.

For once, those powers were not enough. He knew, of course,
that the narrow trail he threaded one afternoon was especially
apt for ambush. But apparently he sensed no "hostiles" till two
arrows sped past his head. Though his Hawken lay across his
saddle, there was only the surer death in his raising it. The
warriors were behind rocks. There was nothing at which he

could shoot. Quickly he studied his circumstance and sized it up as hopeless. He dropped his rifle and raised his hands.

The capture of such a prisoner was a magnificent achievement for The Wolf, the young Blackfoot chief who leaped down now into the trail from a rock above. As his warriors swarmed around him, he danced in jubilant pantomime, then cried in excellent English, "The Killer of Crows has at last been taken."

"All things comes ter pass," his captive replied.

"The Wolf has taken his people's foe."

Johnson shrugged. "I ain't no enemy ter Blackfoots."

The Wolf tapped a knuckle against one of the kegs. "Whiskey!" he said. "Where do you take this whiskey?"

"Ter my frien's the Flatheads. Turn me a-loose, an' . . ."

But Johnson saw already that he had said the wrong thing, that for once his knowledge of the tribes and their enmities had failed him. The Wolf's face froze into a joyous certainty now of what he might do. Hand on thigh, he spat, and his eyes sparkled with hate. "The Flatheads are squaws," he said. "We will bargain for your life with the Crows. Their Killer is doomed."

At The Wolf's order, warriors stripped Johnson of his Crow hunting jacket, his Colt, and his Bowie—but not his flint and steel. Unarmed and naked to the waist, the trapper was driven afoot, and steadily beaten with the flats of tomahawks. At the Blackfoot camp, he was bound with thongs and thrown into a tepee. He was grim, he was angry, and he was contemptuous of this chief who had taken him prisoner. A Crow chief, he thought to himself, would know better than so to humiliate a Liver-Eating Johnson. A Crow chief would either kill such an enemy at once, or set him free.

Methodically, Johnson set to tallying the details of his situation. By his own good luck (and further Blackfoot mismanagement) his hands were fettered in front of him. He would have, it appeared, but one guard and that only a youth. And outside, already, he could hear a rising excitement which could mean but one thing: The Blackfeet were at his whiskey. "Come dark," he

muttered to himself, "an' this coon won't be hyar." Then perhaps, with the guard's knife against what animals he met, and
his own flint and steel against winter's cold. . . .

It was clear from the manner in which his guard eyed Johnson that he had never counted coup. He fingered his long knife
lovingly, in an almost desperate desire to be the warrior who
might take the scalp of the Crow Killer. Then he turned on his
heel, forced himself away from Johnson; he knew that The
Wolf would surely have him killed should he murder so valu-
able a prisoner. And each time that he turned, Johnson sank his
strong teeth into the rawhide thongs that bound his wrists.
Should his guard stare at him too long at a time, Johnson stared
back; the Blackfoot managed a truly ferocious glare, then again
turned away, and Johnson worked a few seconds more at his
thongs.

The late afternoon brought evidence that, despite the increas-
ing din outside, The Wolf was firm in his resolution to sell Johnson, alive. For an old woman came to him with an earthen bowl
of dog, or perhaps muskrat, soup. Telling the story later, Johnson described a dish that was greasy, thick with hair. But offered
such a meal, he made no fastidious complaint; he wolfed it
down to maintain his strength. He relaxed too; Johnson always
could relax when there was no purpose in effort. Arms across his
face, he hunched over his knees as if to sleep. And as he hoped,
his guard increasingly looked away from him toward the entrance, toward the revelry outside. Johnson gnawed away at the
thongs about his wrists.

At last the warrior's desire and Johnson's were satisfied; the
same old woman brought in a pannikin of liquor, then left. As
his guard raised the vessel to swallow, the trapper strained and
burst his bonds. The Indian turned and looked at Johnson derisively, tapped his knife with meaning, then again raised the
whiskey to his lips. At that moment Johnson acted.

The young Blackfoot can hardly have known what struck him.
First he was raised from the ground with a kick that must in

itself have crippled him for fighting. Then as, somehow, he whirled, knife in hand—the pannikin spinning off against the soft wall of the tepee—he took a blow as of a sledgehammer, between the eyes. Any cry he might instinctively have made, was lost in a splutter of whiskey; what moan he did make as he fell was too slight to be heard outside.

Johnson knew he had little time. The old woman might return; there must sometime be a change of guard. Seizing the guard's own knife, Johnson quickly lifted the scalp and tied it to his own belt. Next he slit the buckskin down from the guard's left leg, felt the flesh, ran the knife's keen edge around the hip, and cut to the bone socket. Seizing the knee with one hand and the ankle with the other, he twisted and snapped the whole leg from the body. All was done so deftly that his victim lived.

Johnson stepped quietly into the fast-gathering shadows of night. For a moment he contemplated the band of drunken warriors. Then, the bleeding stump over his shoulder, he stole away. The Blackfeet, when they thought to check on their prisoner, would find only the maimed guard, quivering, stunned, totally incapable of speech.

The weather turned rapidly, bitterly cold. The leg which Johnson carried over his shoulder, gnawed here and there around the hip, was frozen solid. He himself was naked to the waist. He had no real choice of destination, for the Flatheads' camp was three hundred miles ahead of him and his own camp two hundred behind. He must decide, then, whether he had some faint chance of protecting himself from the weather here, in the Owl Creeks, or whether he must cover those two hundred miles.

He was three days in putting the first ten miles between himself and the Blackfoot camp, for while still so close he must cover his trail. In those three days, the snow drove in on him, first sifting in a few large flakes through the utter silence of the wilderness, then howling around him, a mass of cutting, blinding white needles, mounting in the washes, filling gullies and canyons. Johnson crawled against the full blast of the storm to the top of a ridge, then set out southeastward for his camp.

Traveling through the icy mountains by day and crawling into whatever shelter the rocks afforded by night, the Mountain Man lived. Now that the Blackfoot camp was distant, he could warm himself by a fire and thaw out one end of the leg he carried; at least the leg could not go putrid in such weather. He cut what stringy meat he could from it, and spat out the gristle. Then one day on the Sweetwater he hacked at the leg without first putting flame to it, and broke his knife. He threw away the pieces, gnawed, and went on.

One night in the Great Divide Basin he was to discover that he still had one weapon after all. He had found a more than ordinarily comfortable cave. By the fire on its rocky floor, he had for once been able quite to thaw out his emaciated body. His feet to the embers, a firm grip on his victuals, he fell into the sleep of exhaustion.

But in the night he awakened; feeling a tug on his arm, he sat up. Framed in the cave's doorway, against the glistening snow outside, he saw a large mountain lion pulling at the other end of the Blackfoot leg, trying to drag it outside. With a roar the trapper leaped to his feet, tore the leg free, and chased the big cat outside. He was back in the cave soon enough, and again bedding himself down. But now he sensed—heard perhaps—a gaunt grizzly. Presumably the bear had been hibernating in the back recesses of the cave, had been disturbed first by the smoke from Johnson's embers, and had now been angered by the to-do with the cat. The bear advanced on Johnson, and Johnson advanced on the bear; "I warn't," as he was later to tell Del Gue, "in no good humor myself." Swinging his frozen food as a stone-age man his club, the Crow Killer whacked the bear violently across its nose. Now the bear retreated a little, snarling its rage, and Johnson followed up on his advantage. Alternately dodging bear claws and smashing with the leg, he persisted only till the grizzly had had enough. With a last chilling roar the bear turned and trotted, not out of the cave but back to its lair. Johnson left his cave and his hope of a night's sleep, and went on.

Del Gue sat close in the heat of the roaring fire in his rock chimney, mending a broken moccasin and just now clucking, he insisted, at the thought of Johnson's deserting his trap lines to carry whiskey to the Indians. He took a pull at his pipe. He laid his mending aside to listen to the roar of the storm and to watch how the crude latch on his door quivered with the fury of the elements. At last he stood up to tie the rattling thing down. But suddenly the whole door swung open; there in the opening were the wild gust of winter, and Liver-Eating Johnson.

Gue stood, the naked red-bearded giant stood, the doorway between them. Del studied in one long moment the flapping skins that had once been the giant's moccasins and leggings, and the grin on the giant's cadaverous face. Now the giant unslung the frozen thing from his bony shoulder, threw it on the leanto floor, and himself stepped in.

"How air ye fixed fer meat, Del?" said Johnson.

13 Mountain-Man Rendezvous

IT WAS Del Gue who took the winter's furs to Fort Laramie, come spring, and it was he who told the story of Johnson's Blackfoot captivity. Johnson hadn't wanted that story told, it would seem; he must have been pretty weak still, not to make his desire for silence clear to Del. In any event, Del told Johnson's story to Bigfoot Davis, in Laramie trading; and inevitably, when the two had parted, Bigfoot worked the mountain telegraph. Once Bigfoot knew, there was no forestalling a gathering

of the clan. Johnson cussed Del out, when Del said he'd told
Bigfoot; for now he'd have to lead Mountain Men from all the
West against the Blackfeet.[1]

The rendezvous was set for a narrow valley some five miles
east of Virginia City, Montana. There gathered forty of the men
who tore their living from the Rockies by means of rifle, revolver, and Bowie. Some of them had known the trails for
more than half a century; some had ridden with Sublette and
traded furs with Manuel Lisa. Their horses, their saddle blankets, their saddles too showed the range of these men's country
—the tribes among whom they traded, the dead whom they had
plundered. There were men in that gathering who had ridden a
thousand miles for that meeting, each sure that even in such
company he could contribute fighting might. Each was heavily
armed. Some carried as many as four heavy six-shooters, and all
carried their broad Bowie knives in skin sheaths. Their Sharps
and Hawken muzzle-loaders they gripped across the front of
their saddles.

Prominent among them, astride his coal-black mare with the
silky sheen, sat Anton Sepulveda from the Spanish Peaks—six
feet four, his Comanche finery covered with Navajo beadwork,
a trapper as proud of his Spanish heritage as of the fear he commanded from the Colorado to the Mexican Gulf. His flashing
eyes and his tremendous black beard bespoke his volatile nature. His powerful hands, even as he stroked the black's mane,
were those of an unexcelled knife-fighter. Beside Anton Sepulveda, as always, on his half-wild stallion, was José Millardo,
"Apache Joe"; together they had been known to rout an entire

[1] One of those whom Bigfoot told, incidentally, in turn told George
Ogden of Cooke City. George told the story, years later, to Andy Anderson of Andy's Corner, and Andy to George J. McDonald, County Clerk
and Recorder of Red Lodge. McDonald's account is full corroboration
of that narrated by White-Eye Anderson.

village of Apaches, and Anton to pin the chief on his saddle with that sixteen-inch Bowie.

There too sat Anton's competitor Mariano Modeno from the Big Thompson, nimble, sleek, deadly on his dainty-stepping roan gelding. Except on such occasions as this, Mariano Modeno took no partner in his trapping, no partner other than his famous Hawken in his endless killing of Indians; the white teeth between his mustache and his beard gleamed not in pleasure at having company, but in anticipation of blood.

Grizzly Bill Miller, a Missourian astride a fiery Nez Perce pony, fingered the lock on his Hawken. But in fact his knife was the more familiar weapon to him. For Bill Miller, even a mother bear with her cubs was not to be shot from behind a rock but to be tackled face on. Like Bear Claw Chris Lapp—here today too —Bill's business was the gathering of bear claws.

"Señor" Wyatt was there, as quick to kill when challenged as to laugh when entertained—or to tell once again how he won such a name. His taste was for Latin girls; and when he tired of one and dropped her back on her doorstep he swept another onto his saddle and killed what score of fathers, brothers, and cousins might pursue him back toward his hide-out in the San Juans.

Wind River Jake was there, whose back had once been so full of Sioux arrows as "ter look like a porcupine." And Bald Head Pete from the Las Animas, scalped by the Pawnees when still a boy but owner by now of enough Pawnee scalps, as he put it, to roof a cabin. And Mad Mose, another who'd been crudely scalped in the massacre, he said, of all his family—but who, when he could capture an Indian, sometimes cut off his ears and let him live.

There was Jack Ireland, Mose's close friend—"Hatchet Jack," who dismembered and burned his Indian victims piece by piece. Most could think back on some personal tragedy which they must forever avenge. All forty were men supremely to be feared, eager now to pay back the Blackfeet for humiliating Liver-Eating Johnson, for slapping him with tomahawks when his hands were tied. Now they awaited Johnson himself.

Johnson was in Virginia City conferring with John X. Beidler, who had news of The Wolf's whereabouts with his band of Blackfeet. Beidler was willing enough to talk with Johnson alone, but as chief of his town's Vigilantes, he already had his hands full with local outlaws; he insisted that Johnson's forty Mountain Men must stay put. Even so, Grizzly Bill and Big Anton nearly had the forty moving into town when they thought that Johnson had been gone too long. Their preparations to ride on the town were halted only by Johnson's reappearance at the head of the valley.

The Crow Killer who rode toward his forty fellows bore no evident mark of his winter's hardships. Already his huge form was filled out with solid flesh; his fine Crow jacket and leggings fitted him as before. He was mounted on a racing black, and in lieu of his famous matched Colt and Bowie he had a more than adequate brace of Remington .44 six-shooters and a butcher knife as large as a machete.

Johnson's explanation of what he had learned was brief enough: The Wolf's band was "on Willer Crick, by the Three Forks." Some fifty miles due north, then, was the Mountain Men's course. They dismounted to tighten saddle cinches and look to their equipment. Then, with a concerted whoop heard in Virginia City, they remounted and rode toward the Blackfeet.

Every man in that company knew the terrain over which they rode; none need tell the others where they might best look down on the Indian camp. On their third night out, they climbed to a hilltop. There they drew straws to see who should go ahead and scout; the lots fell to Mariano Modeno and Lobo Ned, that half-wild half-breed tracker from Gila River country. Modeno and Ned set aside all but the one essential weapon—their knives—and crept away into darkness. Their companions dismounted and waited, some checking their pistols, others honing knives to razor sharpness, the rest simply staring toward the Blackfoot camp.

Mariano Modeno came back first, with two dripping scalps and the advice that the camp was now wide open to attack.

"How many thar?" Johnson asked.

"Seventy—minus two." Modeno's answer was quiet, yet pronounced so as to carry to all the circle of fighting men. "Viven sesenta y ocho," Big Anton translated for Apache Joe.

Lobo Ned now came out of the darkness, joining the rest only as they mounted their horses. They had expected no further news of him, and he had none; he had found only Modeno's dead sentries.

There was no purpose now in delay. The hour was late. Those who had mufflers for their horses' feet had long since laced them on. Indeed some of the Mountain Men were already on their way to the Blackfoot camp before Johnson gave the word. They moved in remarkable silence, broken but rarely and slightly when a horse's foot struck a rock. Modeno moved forward among them to lead the way and held up only a scant three hundred yards from the camp. Now they regrouped compactly.

Johnson looked at the men who had gathered around him to wipe out his enemies. Señor Wyatt was unconcernedly rolling a cigarette. Big Anton, talking quietly to Apache Joe, twisted gently at his handsome black mustaches. Only Mad Mose glared ferociously ahead, hatchet tight in hand. The Crow Killer struck his mount one smart slap with his open hand. His black pony leaped forward. The blood-curdling yell of the Mountain Men rang as they struck the sleeping camp.

Ten minutes later the trappers had piled wood on the Blackfoot night fires till they lighted up the whole creek bottom. A few Mountain Men were still straggling in with the scalps of Indians whom they had had to chase on foot. But already the camp of The Wolf resembled a slaughterhouse. The bodies of dead Indians lay all around them. There was no sign of serious injury to any of the trappers; only Apache Joe, thrown on rocky soil when his horse stumbled, bore more than a scratch. Liver-Eating Johnson was still to be accounted for, but there was, surely, no real concern to be felt about him. Sixty-nine scalps lay now in a pile for him.

Hours passed. Those many who had knives to clean, cleaned them. Those few who had brought along provisions, ate. Liver-Eating Johnson's forty companions in revenge smoked, talked, and waited for Johnson himself. Their blood lust had not, as so often, been renewed in its very satisfaction; for with none of them injured, none need be avenged.

Just before daylight Johnson finally showed up. His night's conduct was unimpeachable, for under his arm he bore the head of The Wolf and on his belt the scalplock. Over Johnson's shoulder were his own old scabbards, with his famed matched rosewood-handled Walker Colt and Bowie knife.

"Es el fin. Es setenta," Apache Joe said to Big Anton.

And Big Anton turned urgently to his companion. He pointed to a small clump of trees.

Apache Joe was off like a shot, to return a few moments later with a slim box-elder sapling, tidily trimmed and sharpened.

A half-dozen knives were already breaking ground for the planting. Johnson rammed one sharpened end into the loose earth and impaled the head on the other. His companions tamped dirt about the base.

The sun's first long shadows were spotted over the wild, rough land as the Mountain Men finished their task. Only those few who had acted in this last of their ceremony were still afoot; the rest were ready in their saddles. Liver-Eating Johnson looked at the pile of scalps which were his, and Del Gue set to gathering them up. In a moment they two would be alone, but first Johnson must state his thanks. He was obliged, he told his disbanding company, and they should let him know if they ever needed such help from him.

Some of the Mountain Men grunted. Singly or in pairs they rode away toward their own special stamping grounds.

Big Anton Sepulveda and Apache Joe were the last to leave. "No hay más," Johnson told them, "there are no more to kill." "Que lástima," said the huge Anton, more to Joe than to Johnson.

"Usted lo tiene," was Joe's answer. They rode off, turning in their saddles to cry, "Ventura."

Johnson had taken his own private vengeance, against The Wolf. But when today's allies did indeed ask him for help on other such expeditions, against the Sioux or the Nez Perces, they would not leave him so to himself. Having shown them his precision with a skull and a box elder, he would be required to direct the head-poling. He would even be commanded to eat the liver of a Sioux.

14 Boots and Biscuits

BY DEL GUE's account, Liver-Eating Johnson got into the Civil War as soon as the Indians in his stretch of country seemed bent on peace for a while. Johnson put aside his own feud, his reckoning with the twentieth Crow warrior, already twelve years on his trail. (The nineteenth he had killed on La Bonte's Creek, in 1863.) One may decide for oneself what were the full set of motives for Johnson's staying out of the Army as long as he did, and for joining up at the age of forty-one. He knew that the United States was fighting against the "Secesh" or "Rebs." His decision, as the story is handed down, would seem almost too simple: He enlisted when the War seemed to him the best fight going. On February 24, 1864, Johnson and a band of young trappers who'd headed East with him joined the Union Army in St. Louis. They were allowed to keep their side arms but forced to store their Hawkens and use Spencer rifles instead.[1]

The Crow Killer was academically interested enough in a rifle which would fire more than once, but he was naturally leary of a weapon as dangerous to the man who fired it as to the enemy: when it blew up, the entire string of shells in the magazine, housed in the butt, exploded. In his first engagement, Johnson threw his Spencer away and used a dead adversary's single-shot musket.

As a horseman, Johnson was first placed in Company H, Second Colorado Cavalry. His special skills once known, however, he was delegated as sharpshooter and apparently won himself, on this new stage, another reputation.

But Johnson had no such biographer as Del Gue beside him now, and what we know of his nineteen months in the Army reflects amusingly what he thought worth telling Del: the trouble he got into over some scalps. In the third and fourth battles of Newtonia, Missouri, after the great raid of Confederate General Sterling Price had been turned back at Mine Creek, the Union Armies under General J. A. Blunt overtook their foe near Newtonia. The Confederates had already lost many prisoners; now they were saved from utter annihilation only by Shelby's command. Indians fought on both sides in the bloody series of battles, and sharpshooter John Johnston (known also, Veterans Administration records state, as John Johnson) took a vast harvest of Seminole and Cherokee scalps. But while the Seminoles were Confederate soldiers, these Cherokees fought for the Union.

[1] The record of Johnson's Army career, uncovered by F. J. Carey of the Veterans Administration, is skimpy but squares with what Del Gue told White-Eye he had heard from Johnson.

Reprimanded sharply, the Crow Killer gave up his booty and longed for his wilderness.

When the War finally ended, Johnson thought that he would surely be discharged at once. In fact, he had to wait through so long a summer of inactivity that he almost missed the trapping season as well. Somehow, at last he was free. His honorable discharge, again according to VA records, came through on September 23, 1865.[2] Johnson headed north, toward winter.

At a Pawnee encampment on the Platte, he learned that Del was trapping on the Little Medicine Bow, in Wyoming. He traded his blue uniform, cap, and boots to the Pawnee chief Bear That Walks on Two Feet, and received in return a blazed-face black stallion, two suits of new buckskins, a beaver cap, and several pair of moccasins. The buckskins were a pleasure to put on again, but it was the moccasins—after the clumsy discomfort of cavalry boots—which set him to grunting with delight.

Johnson knew from the Pawnees that the Sioux and the Cheyennes, as well as other tribes to the north, were still on the warpath. Already they had massacred party after party of emigrants along the Oregon Trail. But forewarned, he felt forearmed, and in any event he had his Hawken again, fresh out of Army storage, along with the matched Colt and Bowie. The entire Pawnee encampment escorted him across the Platte, and he set out for the Little Medicine Bow.

The real renewal of his adventures took place only some ten miles from Del's camp. Spotting Johnson, four Cheyenne warriors dismounted and stood behind boulders; but disconcertingly, the Crow Killer charged. He had seen one brave, not quite properly hidden; and when the Hawken cracked, that brave pitched forward with a bullet through his neck. Perhaps the three sur-

[2] Letter to R. W. T. from Veterans Administration officials, June 23, 1949.

vivors thought that the dead man had been properly hidden and that Johnson's shot must have curved or miraculously ricocheted. Or perhaps they were simply terrified to see what a fearful foe they had attacked. In any case they leaped to their horses and fled. Johnson went on to Del Gue's camp—and had a more immediate tale to tell than any of the Civil War.

Del, of course, had quantities of news, most of it bad. The Apaches had killed Apache Joe, and in endless lust for revenge Big Anton was exterminating them as, once, Johnson himself had slaughtered Crows. Bigfoot Davis had fallen to the Snakes, on the far side of the mountains. "Señor" Wyatt too was dead, riddled with lead, after fighting it out at his lone camp in the San Juans against "half ther Greasers atween hyar an' ther Pecos"; his head had been carried off on a pole. And in the coming flare-up of savage fighting, Johnson's own life was once again especially to be challenged. The Blackfeet, Del told him, had decided that "Any brave whut kin tek yer hair is ter be made a chief."

Astonishingly, Johnson's first weeks home were quiet and relaxed. The Liver-Eater would not believe that Blackfeet could do what his great foes the Crows could not. He and Del worked their trap lines incessantly and peaceably throughout the winter, with excellent luck. Their only unfriendly visitor was the twentieth and last of the Crows long since marked to kill Johnson. Even that adventure was not in Johnson's usual heroic mold, for he was almost caught off guard, washing dishes.

Now the Crow Killer was noted throughout the Mountains for his skill in baking biscuits; and one morning in early March, when the partners were already considering taking in their sets for the winter, he decided to make enough biscuits to last till they should leave camp. Since there was only one large pan in camp, he spent most of the day at his amiable chore. The last batch was baked only along about mid-afternoon. In the last warmth of the daytime, Johnson ambled to the riverbank to scour the pan before packing it away. Fortune and, of course, instinct were with him. Bent over as he was, he could not be seen from the camp site. But as he worked away on the pan with cloth and sand, he sensed—smelled, as he put it—a familiar foe.

Humping along in squatting position to a clump of dried grass, the trapper could peer toward his camp. There he saw a gigantic Crow warrior stuffing biscuit after biscuit into his mouth yet scanning his horizon constantly, a naked knife in hand. Quietly setting his frying pan on the ground, Johnson crept stealthily along the riverbank, his plan of action already in mind.

Now despite the Crow's vigilance, Johnson could easily have shot from behind the shelf of the riverbank or from behind his clump of dried grass. But he was concerned as much with making good his desire that every Crow must know the manner of his death, as with effecting the death itself. The Crow Killer must, then, stalk his quarry. He waded with utmost caution past the shelf and to a slope out of sight from the biscuits.

Before Johnson could reach him, the warrior had time pretty well to spoil the week's planned catering. Then suddenly, as he stooped for yet another biscuit, he was propelled violently upward. Even as he was in the air he must have sensed what enemy had so surprised him, for though he came down balancing on the balls of his feet and whirled, knife in hand, he had already begun his death song. He could not have begun later. The Crow Killer's Bowie was at once buried in his chest.

Johnson spared Del Gue another witnessing of his rites with the liver, but of course the biscuits he was warming "for Del's supper" when his partner returned, were precisely those stained by the dead Crow's blood; the Crow's mutilated body still lay by the fire.

"Nothin' fer me, Liver-Eatin'," Del begged. "I kilt me a couple o' sage hens down river."

"Sage hens, my foot," said Johnson; and for a time he insisted on detailing his own supper of warm biscuits and warm liver. But at last, letting up on his partner, he fell silent; and Del could reflect.

"Good God!" said Del. "This'n air number twenty."

Johnson nodded.

"On yer trail fer ten y'ars!"

"Near fourteen," Johnson told him.

Struck by the similarity of their thought, the partners fell to discussing the Crows. Even more admirable than Crow hardihood, they agreed, was Crow tenacity. For a warrior to spend so many years away from his family, on such a death trail, was marvelous indeed. The partners spoke of how many times he must surely have hidden near his village, to spy upon his family and watch his children grow. They considered, too, how as one by one the others of the chosen twenty died, loneliness must have come upon him more and more; for three years now there had been no fellow tribesman to whom he could speak. He had grown accustomed, no doubt, to warding off for himself all physical hunger and cold; but the hunger and cold in his soul must have passed all bounds.

It was Del who said, "I'm shore glad that's over." He stared bleakly at the brawny corpse before them and traced the slit in the abdomen with a dried weed.

Even Johnson had no more fun to make of his partner's queasiness. Quietly he cut the twentieth notch in the rosewood handle of his Bowie.

Del apparently felt he must say some good word for his partner's special habit. "They's a doctor at ther Fort says liver gives people stren'th," he said.

"Never hurt nobody," the Liver-Eater agreed, but he turned the conversation more or less away from the day's blood: "I'll be bakin' biscuits ag'in, t'morrer."

15 Portuguese Phillips

IN THE year 1866 the greatest concentrations of hostile Indians ever seen in the West began a series of military engagements and massacres that lasted into the early 1870's. Eventually, just as he had been drawn into the Civil War, Johnson would find himself swept into the general fighting. Yet ideally, to Johnson's way of thinking, even such enemy strength should be met by the might and the guile of individual Mountain Men. Army forces might be necessary to protect settlers, but when a detachment of soldiers was surrounded and helpless before the Indian foe, there must be one Mountain Man, a Portuguese Phillips, say, to get through and report the soldiers' plight. Johnson's real reverence for individual achievement and his concern for the legend appear strikingly in the help he gave Phillips, and his effort to hide that help from men's knowledge. If Phillips recounted how his ride through blizzard waste, glorious as it was, would have ended in disaster without Johnson's help—why, Johnson had done what he could to make the adventure seem Phillips' alone.[1]

The Sioux, especially, were on the warpath, and they drew into their fighting orbit the Cheyennes, the Arapahos, the Blackfeet, and for a time some Crows. The Sioux were thus the leaders of all those tribes who came to feel that if so many white men came now to settle among them, then already they meant to seize all the lands of the vast West for themselves. Thus the

[1] Doc Carver confirms Johnson's friendship with Phillips (Carver mss., p. 17): "I ran into a fellow at Fort McPherson who had been an Indian scout in the north; his name was Phillips. He was to guide a detachment of soldiers up the trail to a northern fort. We asked him about the buffalo herds in Wyoming, and he said he had never seen such big herds. He said he had killed buffalo for the army post [probably Laramie] and that Liver-Eating Johnson and some other hunters had gone with him."

Indians could lose nothing by resisting. Every settlement was attacked or in fear of attack. Every trail was an Indian target.

Along the Bozeman Trail in Wyoming, for example, whites were massacred by the hundreds. On July 15, 1866, Colonel H. B. Carrington, 18th United States Infantry, and his command reached a point some sixty-five miles north of the deserted Fort Reno and there built Fort Phil Kearny in the very heart of Red Cloud's Sioux domain. Red Cloud had had promises from Washington that no whites would be stationed or allowed to settle in his territory. As early as July 17, his warriors ran close to the fort site and drove off some stock. "There never was an hour" in all the building and active maintenance of the "Hated Fort on the Little Piney" when the Sioux did not post their warriors about it (and indeed, when the fort was at last left empty, they "rushed in and set fire to all the buildings and stockade" with the soldiers only three miles away.[2]

Now the fort seemed well situated for defense, on a plateau between the Little Piney Creek and the Big Piney. But those within its walls must face not only the Sioux but also the cold of winter—one of the coldest winters, as was to develop, in the history of Wyoming. The two hundred and fifty who were to man the fort, accordingly, must include some fifteen woodcutters. Red Cloud determined to strike at the woodcutters first, but in such a manner as to draw the soldiers from inside their fortifications. He was determined to destroy every man and woman and child in the fort, but in order to do so he must let one woodcutter escape.

What seemed a mere hunting party of Sioux, accordingly, fell on the woodcutters. The one survivor, reaching the fort, told his story to Colonel Carrington and Carrington's lieutenant, Captain William J. Fetterman. Fetterman, a valiant soldier, at once urged that the Sioux hunting party must be punished. Carrington gave him the permission he sought, but with this qualifica-

[2] Major A. B. Ostrander, *After Sixty Years* (Seattle: Gateway Printing Co., 1925), p. 82.

tion: He must not go beyond Lodge Pole Ridge. Quickly gathering a troop of some eighty soldiers, both infantry and cavalry, Fetterman marched over the snowy plain toward the woods.

There were no Indians to be seen. When he reached Lodge Pole Ridge in quiet, Fetterman decided that if he were to give the red men a lesson he must follow them further. He ordered his infantrymen to ride double on the mounts of the cavalrymen. In fact, the infantrymen could easily have marched as much further as they were to go. Fetterman and his eighty rode over the ridge and into a small clearing in a depression. The landscape all around erupted. A thousand Sioux fell upon them.

The massacre that followed has won a reputation as more macabre than any other of its sort, just as Red Cloud himself has won a name among the fiercest of Indian warriors and, along with the great Oglala Sioux, Crazy Horse, as the greatest of Indian strategists. There were no survivors. The dead were mutilated beyond recognition. Many were clubbed until "every bone" in their bodies was broken. Such was the answer of Red Cloud to the encroachment of the Army.

Colonel Carrington was now left with a pitifully small garrison to meet the attack that Red Cloud would surely soon be making. Even so, he would order no soldier to go for help. The nearest possible reinforcements were at Fort Laramie, 236 miles away—236 miles, that is to say, after a courier got through the Sioux warriors ringing the fort. The Indians would, of course, be expecting a courier. They would be ready to ambush him on every trail. No soldier had the hardihood for such a trip anyway, in weather twenty-five degrees below zero. No soldier could have found the way in the constant snows, but would have frozen to death in the wilderness. Colonel Carrington asked for volunteers but can hardly have been surprised when only a Mountain Man stepped forward, John "Portuguese" Phillips.

Phillips was a tall, heavily bearded scout with extraordinary qualifications for the assignment. The several Indian languages at his command were but one proof of how well he knew the tribesmen themselves. His trigger finger was respected by all the hostiles. He knew all the rocks and gullies near the Bozeman Trail, not simply as rugged or picturesque scenery but for the possibilities of ambush they afforded. Said the scout to the Colonel, "All I wants is the best hoss on the post, an' my saddlebags full o' biscuits."

Said the Colonel to the scout, "You may have my horse, Phillips, and anything else you may need."

Phillips knew well enough which was the best horse on the post. The Colonel's chestnut Arabian was often called the best piece of horseflesh in the entire West. And Carrington must have known he would never see the horse again. Even should Phillips get through, he must surely be able to do so only by pushing to the very limit of the animal's endurance, and then beyond.

Perhaps in dramatization of the circumstances which could force him to give up such a horse, Carrington issued an order as Phillips left. All the women and children were to remain constantly in the arsenal. The soldier there in charge must touch match to powder, should the Indians gain entrance to the stockade. Clearly, if Red Cloud should strike before reinforcements could come, the fort must fall.

Portuguese Phillips completed his preparations for the ride before dark on the day after the twin massacres. His biscuits, fresh-baked, were stowed in his bags. His horse, saddled and bridled by an orderly with Carrington himself looking on, was led to the gate. Carrington had prevailed upon him to wear an Army coat. The scout himself had checked and rechecked his own arms: two Colt revolvers, a Bowie knife, and a Spencer repeating rifle (more reliable now than the model issued, only two years before, to Johnson). John C. Brough, the sentry, told later how the Colonel came with Phillips to the gate and stroked for a moment the silken mane of his thoroughbred. "May God be with you," he said softly to Phillips. The scout gathered up the reins, nudged the chestnut, and slipped through the opening and out upon the Bozeman Trail. He had embarked on a ride as lonely and terrible as any in military history—as terrible in its way as Liver-Eating Johnson's forced march had been, on his way from Blackfoot captivity.

Phillips did not stick to the Bozeman Trail, for he could count on the Indians' patrolling that now-deserted artery all the way to Fort Reno and even beyond. He paralleled the road wherever he could, but anywhere from two to five miles away. The snow had stopped falling for the last few hours before he left the fort, and he could ride for a time at a stiff canter. But after he had been in the saddle for two hours or so, such heavy flakes came down as very nearly obscured the horse's head; he held a loose rein now and let the animal pick its way. From time to time he had to slow the great thoroughbred down to a trot or even, so rough was the going, to a walk. Both man and beast felt the temptation to all possible speed in such cold, but they could afford no crippling tumble, no laming near-fall. Phillips felt the night's cold grow ever sharper. His chin was already muffled in his Army coat; now and again he tried to shrug yet further into its collar.

If there was any one ambush the Sioux would assuredly have set for him, that one certainly would be at Crazy Woman's Fork of the Powder River; here he left the trail altogether. By midnight he knew that he was more than halfway to Fort Reno, and so perhaps one seventh of his way to Laramie. He made a camp in the lee of a cliff, though he knew he could afford no rest himself. He took off the saddle and the wet blanket, rubbed the Arabian down, and put one of his own dry blankets on the animal. He set out a few mouthfuls of the grain he carried in a sack, made coffee in his pannikin over a small fire—at least the heavy snow made that luxury safe—and ate some biscuits. Then he melted some snow for the horse. After a half hour's respite he saddled up, kicked out and buried all traces of his fire, and went on.

The cold stunned him now, it seemed, more than before his rest; the darkness was if anything more impenetrable. This Army horse could not judge the difference between a snow drift and a hillock covered with snow, and Phillips must keep alert every moment. On level stretches he could let the thoroughbred stretch his limbs. In broken country he must judge at each step what the animal was getting into.

That night did pass. Around four in the morning, Phillips saw the black blob which was the deserted Fort Reno. Here he could allow himself and his horse a two-hour rest. Again he groomed and fed the horse. When they set out once more, the dark had not lifted, yet they felt refreshed. As they rode across the plain into the slow coming of daylight, the horse seemed as lively as at the start of the ride.

Through the second day, the weather was less severe, and Phillips' problem was simply how much he could ask of the horse. With no fresh snowfall and a wind gentle enough to leave the night's snow on the ground, the wilderness stretched before the scout interminably. He set the horse into a mile-eating gallop. All day long he rode, conserving his mount only when the footing was less sure, and taking only one short hour's rest. When night fell on them they had passed Salt Creek, and Phillips could set his course for Fort Casper.

That night had two surprises for Portuguese Phillips. The first surprise was his steed's stamina. Each hour that passed he felt sure that now he must stop and make camp; each hour the horse stood up so well that again he postponed such delay. At last, near midnight, Phillips decided that whatever the horse's appearance of continued strength, both must have some rest. Though he saw no certain landmark, he knew he was nearing the Overland Trail and estimated that he must have ridden almost halfway to Laramie. Observing a clump of snow-covered willows near a creek, he rode toward them.

Phillips' second surprise was the sound of voices—Sioux, he assumed. Surely no large body of warriors could be camped in the willows; or perhaps, half frozen and tired almost to the point of falling from his horse, Phillips felt he might as well take on whatever of Red Cloud's fighting forces were here. Taking the reins in his teeth and cocking his rifle, he rode straight into the clump, observing as he passed the fringe the roaring fire ahead of him.

Two white men stood by the fire. Even in such a moment, Phillips smelled the aroma of a pot of coffee. The two men stood before their makeshift fireplace, rifles pointed straight at the scout's head.

It was Liver-Eating Johnson who broke the silence. A bit sheepishly, he introduced Phillips and "X" Beidler, then asked, "Whar air ye from, Portygee?"

And when Phillips, it seemed, could not at once reply, Johnson lifted him from the saddle as gently as if he had been a baby (though taking care to loosen Phillips' frozen gauntlet from the ready trigger of his rifle). Beidler—who, as Vigilante chief of Virginia City, had directed the forty Mountain Men to The Wolf's Blackfoot camp—threw some antelope steaks on the coals beside the coffeepot. Johnson poured Phillips his first cup of coffee. And at last the courier could give them the news of the massacres at Fort Phil Kearny, and his own mission.

While Beidler cared for the horse, in truth nearly exhausted, Johnson moved the fire and spread blankets on the warm earth where it had been. "Now, Portygee," he said, "ye air a-goin' ter rest an' sleep."

Phillips protested that he could not, that every hour he could save he must save.

"I'll wake yer up when the time comes. We is jist from Laramie, an' I'll make up yer sleepin' time with short cuts."

And Phillips did indeed sleep, after his coffee and steaks. Some two hours before daylight, he was awakened by Johnson's nudge. He sprang to his feet and saw before him two saddled horses, his own mount and the Crow Killer's powerful black. "I'll jist show Portygee over ther rough parts," Johnson said as if addressing only Beidler. "Watch yer scalp." The two men mounted and were almost at once on their way.

At daybreak they looked ahead over a country dead and barren and cold—what each had seen for a generation of winters in this wilderness. Johnson's breath turned his great beard into a solid block of ice. The northwest wind, starting up now, almost swept the horses off their feet. Yet there was reason to be grateful even for such a wind when Johnson turned their course to the southeast, and thus put the wind behind them. "We air plenty below Casper now," he told Phillips. The scout nodded.

Taking advantage of their tail wind, they put their horses into a gallop, to thunder across vast plains from which the snow had been swept by the gales. When they judged the time to be noon, they rode their mounts into a deep dry wash and made a short camp. Phillips knew that their short cuts had already saved him any time lost in last night's sleep, and this must be their last rest. Johnson produced more antelope steak from his saddlebags, and Phillips furnished the last of his biscuits along with a pannikin of coffee. Phillips saw how closely Johnson studied the Arabian as both horses were unsaddled and rubbed down, their blankets warmed over the fire and replaced. When at last both horses and men had eaten, they had one brief exchange about Phillips' chances.

"It's a hunderd miles ter Laramie. If yer hoss makes it," Johnson said.

"Oh, I think we'll make out," Phillips answered.

Both men felt, as they rose to saddle once again, how during their hour's rest the wind had risen, bringing promise of a blizzard. Johnson saw no reason now for sparing even the Arabian. They thundered ahead at a stiff gallop, hoping to stay ahead of the storm. Within four hours they reached the Platte and found it frozen to its bottom. The river furnished them an excellent trail, so they kept to its right bank for more than forty miles.

But when they were perhaps twenty miles from Laramie, Johnson surprised Phillips by ordering a halt. Once more they built a small fire, in the lee of the river bank. Once more, as they thawed themselves out, the Crow Killer inspected the Arabian.

"This hoss is about done," he said.

"I still think we'll make it," Phillips answered him.

"Ye kin, Portygee. But ye better tek it easy."

Phillips looked at Johnson with astonishment. "Ain't ye a-goin' on in with me?" he asked.

Johnson shook his head. "Plenty might like to, but not this coon," he said, and busied himself over the fire, knocking the last icicles to earth from his beard. "Ye see, Portygee, this ride'll make hist'ry fer ye."

The two shook hands, mounted their horses, and rode away, Phillips for Laramie and Johnson back over the trail they had come together.

The blizzard fell furiously upon Laramie, this Christmas Eve. The swirling snow started once more to mount over the already deep-covered prairies. Once again the temperature fell, to forty below now. The wind howled down out of the frozen north. The sentry walking his gate post, his lips chapped and cut even though he clung to the lee side of the stockade, thought what it must be like in the open—thought that no man could live long in the storm outside. Then he knew, suddenly, that the sound at the gate was not of wind alone. He swung the gate wide. A rider urged his horse, braced against the wind, on slowly into the courtyard.

The sentry, even as he closed and barred the gate, saw the gaunt, stiff rider dismount. After a few more halting steps, the animal fell. The sentry saw the rider stagger up the steps toward the door of the post's Bedlam House, where the officers and their wives danced on this holiday eve. Portuguese Phillips twisted open the door, pointed to his breast pocket, and then like his horse fell forward.

The messages Phillips carried, in three days' ride, served their vital purpose; reinforcements reached Fort Phil Kearny before Red Cloud could strike. The first of Colonel Carrington's messages, to the General who could send him immediate help, read thus:

Fort Phil Kearny, Dec. 21st, 1866
By Courier to Fort Laramie

Gen. P. St. Geo. Cooke:
Do send me reinforcements forthwith. Expedition, now with my force, impossible. I risk everything but the post and its stores. I venture as much as any one can but I have had today a fight unexampled in Indian warfare. My loss is ninety-four (94) killed. I have recovered forty-nine (49) bodies, and thirty-five (35) more are to be brought in in the morning. I need prompt reinforcements and repeating arms. I am sure to have an active winter and must have men and arms. Promptness is the vital thing. Give me officers and give me men.

The second of the messages Phillips carried from Carrington was to General U. S. Grant and proposed not defense but a remounted offense.

General: I want all my officers. I want men. Depend upon it, as I wrote in July, no treaty, but hard fighting, is to assure this line—but to open and guarantee this line I must have reinforcements and the best of arms.

As those notes were first read, in Fort Laramie, Liver-Eating Johnson rode head on into the storm. His powerful black snapped and bit at the snowflakes' sting. His thoughts were, surely, with Phillips; but just what he may have thought about Phillips we cannot know. Perhaps he was sure enough of his own estimate of man and horse alike, to know that Phillips would have by now made it to Laramie. Or perhaps he merely hoped Phillips might have made it—and thought Phillips' chance for glory worth risking the lives of the hundred and fifty still manning an Army fort

The rigors of that extraordinary winter were too harsh for another of the mountain people, Mrs. John Morgan—Crazy Woman. Along with the provisions Liver-Eating Johnson and some few of his friends brought her, Crazy Woman depended on what game she could shoot. That winter, it seems, she went blind from a blow she had received from the Blackfeet who descended upon all her family twenty years before. Early in the spring that came at last, Johnson heard that the old woman had starved to death.

16 A Sioux Liver

EVEN SO confirmed an individualist as Liver-Eating Johnson must share in such a defense of settlers' women and children as that at Fort Hawley, in 1869. His distinctive contribution, however, the eating of a Sioux liver, was by way of a command performance required by those very Mountain Men who had "helped" him to a vengeance against the Blackfeet.

Fort Hawley—named for an Army man and fur wholesaler who never saw the place—was a trading post and rendezvous for hunters and trappers from all the far West. In 1869 it was in charge of one Captain Andrews and his small detachment of soldiers. Johnson, arriving on routine business, found there a number of settlers who had been driven from their homes by the Sioux. Many of their people had been killed, and the smoke and flames of burning cabins were to be seen along all that stretch of the Missouri. Already many Mountain Men had offered their help, among them Del Gue and his last-winter's partner Jim Deer. Beidler was there, and hoary-headed Bear Claw Chris Lapp. Bear Claw had pretty much retired from violence, settling down instead to the sale of his special necklaces to an excellent new market—the "tenderfeet" on river steamboats; but he had come out from his cabin in the Little Rockies for the present emergency. Hatchet Jack Ireland was in the band as well, with his adopted "father," Mad Mose.

The few soldiers present kept themselves in the stockade, some fifty yards from the trading post. Johnson, like the rest of the Mountain Men, camped outside where they had "stompin' room." While keeping a lookout for hostiles, they repaired their gear or fished in the muddy Missouri; at times indeed, such contempt had they for their foe, they let their guard down altogether. Each knew himself worth more than a company of soldiers, in this countryside so familiar to them.

In the quiet weeks they whiled away, a number of other trappers came in. One, the famous Indian fighter George Grinnell, reported that there was no sign of Indians anywhere near. Then two days after Grinnell brought such word, Johnson and Del Gue, fishing from cottonwood stumps on the riverbank, heard a woman's scream.

Seizing their rifles, they ran to the top of the river, and on toward where they had seen two women picking Juneberries in the brush, one white, the other Indian. The white woman, Jennie Smith, was still lying where she had been scalped alive; the Indian woman, racing toward the fort, was hit in the buttocks by a shot from the now retreating foe. Other Mountain Men too were racing toward the scene. Their short examination showed that Jennie Smith had suffered no harm other than the loss of her scalp (and indeed Beidler's manuscripts show that the woman lived many years, with a wig to cover her only wound). A pan of water thrown into her face revived her.

Johnson, the story runs, wasted some two minutes in cussing himself out for believing Grinnell's story—"I been a-smellin' them Sioux fer an hour"—but in a moment's time the chase was on. There was a willow belt running parallel with the river, through which the Sioux tried to escape. But the Indians had not reconnoitered enough. Pressed close, and fearing the deadly aim of the Mountain Men, they dropped into a dry wash at the end of the timber. The wash was blind; they were boxed. Their only hope was that the trappers would leave the timber and run toward them, easy targets. But the Mountain Men knew that they had the Sioux trapped and that not one of them could leave the wash alive. Johnson and the rest need only wait until near dark, to make their move.

Through the remaining hours of daylight, the Sioux seemed to take some amusement from the Mountain Men's deadly aim. Again and again they thrust their coup sticks above the rim of the wash—as if in admission that those sticks would never again be of use to them. Again and again their sticks were shot cleanly in two.

Come twilight, Johnson and Del Gue crawled on their bellies through the small willow scrub at the end of the wash. They discovered that the Indians had barricaded their position with heavy shields made from the neck skin of bull buffalos, and hung blankets to keep the Mountain Men from taking aim.

Had the trappers still carried their old light-calibered Hawken rifles or even the heavier Spencer repeaters, the shields might have effectively turned their bullets. But instead each man carried the hardest-hitting rifle ever seen on the western plains —the .56 caliber Springfield, known as a needle gun because the firing pin, several inches in length, ran through the heaviest breech block ever built into a rifle. The three-ounce lead bullet from this gun, with its heavy powder charge, would go right through a running buffalo.

Del crawled back to the heavy timber to report. Soon the entire band of whites was lined up before the mouth of the wash for what would clearly be nothing more than a riddling of the Sioux. Their first volley killed more than a third of the Indians. The rest, realizing at once that they must die, began singing their death songs. Then, gracefully conceding to superior fire power, they climbed the rim of the wash and were felled. One of them, not killed but lying with both hips smashed by a single bullet, sang while Jim Deer approached him, placed muzzle to his head, and pulled the trigger. But because the caps on the muzzle-loader were wet, Deer snapped all around the cylinder without effect. At last he picked up a stone with which to dash out the warrior's brains, but Johnson, intervening, shot the Indian dead.

There was little celebrating to be done after such a massacre, aside from the usual collection of scalps and other valuables. But Hatchet Jack did conceive what might entertain his fellows. "Ever chaw on a Sioux nigger's liver, Liver-Eatin'?" he asked.

The other Mountain Men, gathering round, left Johnson no alternative but to "chaw"—or to suggest that his liver-eating was only legend. In wordless answer, he stooped over the Sioux he had just killed. Soon he had the liver in his hands. Del Gue alone, it seems, turned away in disgust. Holding the trophy for all to see, Johnson sank his teeth into the dripping flesh.

"I kin see how ye earned yer name," said George Grinnell.

"Great Jehosophat, Pocahontas, an' John Smith," old Bear Claw cried out at the suggestion that there had ever been any doubt. "He wuz eatin' 'em way back in Hatcher's time."

Johnson spat out some gristle. "Del don't like it," he said, "makes him gag."

Johnson never did finish that last of the livers he ate. He turned aside, instead, to direct the boiling down of the thirty-two skulls, for mounting on poles. Peter Koch, in his journal, reports the effect on the passengers of the steamer *Huntsville*, landing at Fort Hawley some days later:

A sight met her passengers which was certainly calculated to shock the nerves of any eastern tenderfoot. Along the brink of the river bank on both sides of the landing a row of stakes was planted, and each stake carried a white, grinning Indian skull. They were evidently the pride of the inhabitants, and a little to one side, as if guarding them, stood a trapper, well-known throughout eastern

Montana by the soubriquet of 'Liver-Eating' Johnson. He was leaning on a crutch, with one leg bandaged, and the day being hot his
entire dress consisted of a scant, much shrunken, red undershirt,
reaching just below his hips. His matted hair and bushy beard flut-
tered in the breeze, and his giant frame and limbs, so freely exposed
to view, formed an exceedingly impressive and characteristic picture.[1]

"X" Beidler, writing of the same occasion in his Journal manuscripts, and incidentally erring as to the date, suggested the
Sioux liver was the first eaten by Johnson. But then the stories
invented about Johnson's liver-eating were often ludicrously off
the mark. Take S. D. Shackleford's, for example, as passed on
by Pack-Saddle Ben Greenough:

In 1873 two young men met in St. Louis, John Johnston and
John A. Mann. [Johnston had, of course, been in the West for thirty
years by 1873, and was no longer really young.] Proceeding on
his journey [to the West] Johnston went first to a town named
Coulson on the Yellowstone. [In fact, the young Coulson for whom
Coulson was named was not born until 1879 and was not brought
to the new town until 1880. Shackleford's story itself has "young"
Johnston failing to kill his first Indian until 1882, nine years after
the boast to "A. Mann." By 1882, the real Johnson was almost
sixty.] In 1882 when Billings had replaced Coulson,[2] a young tenderfoot arrived in town. This tenderfoot, who wore yellow button shoes,
straw hat, seersucker coat, and linen duster, was allowed by Johnston to go on a scouting trip with him to the Snowy [Big Snow]
Mountains. Johnston killed two Indians, and when the tenderfoot
[who had apparently been in hiding] appeared, the scout cut the
liver from one, rubbed it on his face, and the young man got sick.

[1] Sanders, *History of Montana*, I, 234.
[2] "The history of Coulson was a matter of a few years, 1879 to perhaps 1883 or 1884. With the building of the Northern Pacific railroad
and the selection of Billings as the site for the town the days of Coulson
were numbered." Letter from Mrs. Anne McDonnell of the Historical
Society of Montana to R. W. T., dated Helena, April 24, 1950.

We may pass over those other stories of how Johnston or Johnson earned his name, as cited already in the Acknowledgments. We may go on to how—just before eating that one Sioux liver—the Crow Killer made peace with the Crow. We may then tell how, even in the bitter warfare against the Sioux, Liver-Eating Johnson kept largely aside from such debauchery in blood as he had been engaged in near Fort Hawley.

17 Monument for a Foe's Friend

IN THE winter of 1868–69, the Crow Killer and "X" Beidler, having no commitments to the military, resolved to set out trapping. After months on scouts' pay, they were pinched financially. More important, they would break the monotony of hanging around Army posts. Instead of setting out for any of the richest fur fields, they went to Beidler's comfortable cabin in the Big Belt Mountains. Though glad of the privacy of one another's company, they worked assiduously, and surprisingly enough they did bring in a good winter's haul.

Thus the two came out of the Belts in March with two pack horses heavily loaded. Their winter's lonely activity, the spring's freshness, and the very sort of scrape they met with Blackfeet, all were as simple as in young John Johnston's first seasons in the West twenty-five years ago. That was before the coming of so many settlers, before such intensive posting of Army detachments, before the determined uprising of the Sioux and their friends. The snow melted in the mountains as Johnson and Beidler rode along the river sides. The willows and cottonwoods stretched their just-unburdened limbs. Small parties of Crows and Blackfeet were on their springtime move, some to trade and others to kill, or more likely all of them to see what adventures they might meet.

It was twenty young Blackfoot warriors, seeking to make a name for themselves by gathering white scalps, who followed the trail of the two trappers. When they came close enough to see their quarry's packs of furs, they must have been certain they would gain both wealth and fame. What they did not know, any more than had some of their tribesmen a generation earlier, was that the prosperous trappers were not as sleepy as they looked. Johnson had smelled them out on the first day of their trailing. As Beidler remarked, "If'n them red devils knew who they wuz trailin', they'd be makin' tracks t'other way." The two Mountain Men waited only for ground the Blackfeet would think apt for ambush, to prepare their own.

There would be no moon. The ground they chose, for their own encampment and for the Blackfoot descent upon them, was the famous camping site on the forks near the headwaters of the Musselshell, west of Pompey's Pillar. At the confluence of the left fork and the river itself, they made such a fire that not even the least experienced party of raiders could miss them, such a fire indeed that any but fledglings must expect a trap. The smoke from the trappers' green brush and young spring shoots could be seen for miles; the dry driftwood they added would keep the fire going. As dusk came on, the trappers tethered their horses safely away from the fire, walked back a few feet along the trail, then posted themselves one on either side in the rocks and the brush. Each had a new improved Spencer repeater and two revolvers. An hour passed, two, three. (The Blackfeet had dismounted a mile from the forks and were creeping forward, spread out along both sides of the trail, but as yet even Johnson had heard no sound of them.) Soon the "campfire" would have burned out. Soon, on this moonless night, there would be no light by which foe could be seen.

"Hyar they come, X." Beidler heard his partner's low voice

from across the trail, at last. He had expected that Johnson
would remark the young Blackfeet's coming first. But even now
that Johnson had alerted him, he could hear nothing more
than the crackling and hissing of the dry logs burned almost
through. He cuddled his rifle stock against his cheek and took
comfort from his certainty that across the trail Liver-Eating
Johnson stood in identical position. He gazed down the trail. At
last he saw shapes darting, at long intervals, from rock to rock.
These young Indians had been well trained in stealth and camou-
flage. Now Beidler, like Johnson, must wait till they came to
some impasse for which they had not been trained. Beidler
had the benefit of Johnson's training in how they might best
take advantage of this terrain, but even so he resolved to let
Johnson's rifle speak first.

At last one young brave, evidently the leader and bolder than
the others, stepped out and advanced to the campfire; Beidler
was close enough to see the Indian's black eyes gleam in the
firelight. Drawing no attack upon himself, he set the butt of his
rifle on the ground and raised one hand in the air. Now suddenly
and silently the lighted space about the campfire was filled
with twenty eager young warriors. (Most carried rifles; Beidler
could imagine what Johnson would have to say about traders
who would sell the tribes so many rifles that even young men
like these had firearms.) The leader gesticulated, pointing
toward where the trappers had led their horses away from the
fire. All his men came close to hear what he had to say. Now
the rifles opened up on them from both sides of the trail.

The party of Blackfeet was caught dead between the two well-
hidden trappers. Most of the braves fell in the first burst of
lead upon them. Before the remaining few could think what
action to take, Johnson and Beidler had emptied their rifles and
were among them with revolvers. One did manage to slash
Beidler's shoulder with his scalping knife, but of the other
Blackfeet even those who had scant time to raise rifle or fit
arrow to bow had no time for accurate aim. Three only of the

full score made their escape, and Johnson was sure that two of these were badly wounded.

But with even three escaped into the darkness, Johnson and Beidler must move away from their "campfire." Soon the entire Blackfoot nation would be alerted against them. More immediately, they must stay away from this light which had made the Blackfeet their helpless targets. They did have two, perhaps three, minutes for Johnson to take seventeen scalps, with Beidler standing guard. They did, no doubt, take along the foe's rifles. ("Yer see even these young 'uns hez rifles?" Johnson asked; and Beidler answered that he did.) But in little more than five minutes the trappers were on horseback, headed for water. Even the packing of Beidler's shoulder wound, in herbs from Johnson's saddlebags, must wait till they had followed the river where it was shallow, and crossed and recrossed several times.

When daylight came, the trappers found Johnson's old trapping cabin, hidden in its dense underbrush. They spent the hours till dark there, sleeping and watching turn and turn.

On the second night's ride after their massacre of the Blackfeet, the trappers entered a belt of heavy timber. Beidler had not Del Gue's knowledge of this Musselshell country, nor for that matter Del's knack of drawing from Johnson some statement of plans; but when he found himself riding behind Johnson single file along this well-worn trail, even Beidler remembered what his partner might be doing in this country. "By God," he said, "this air the trail ter Crazy Woman's place."

Johnson allowed that Beidler was right but made no further reply. They rode out of the timber and into the clearing. They dismounted by what was obviously an empty cabin, and the Crow Killer led the way past the cabin to Mrs. Morgan's four mounds, still clearly marked but long unattended. Wind and water had turned them awry. The four poles still stood at the corners of the little graveyard, but they were no longer adorned with skulls. The Crow Killer walked on past to a fifth grave, off to one side, under a huge cairn of stones eight feet or more in height.

"You knowed she wuz dead?" Beidler asked.

"I knowed," Johnson said; and he did explain to Beidler how she had died of starvation. He walked around her cairn. He stopped to inspect the four poles set around this grave as around the graveyard the old woman had tended herself, and to mark the four cracked, grinning skulls set thereon. "Crows piled up these stuns," he said matter-of-factly.

"Why not Blackfoots?"

"Blackfoots hated her, an' wuz skeered ter come hyar."

The trappers had remounted before Beidler pursued the matter. "But why the Crows?" he asked then.

The Liver-Eater took a chew of tobacco. "Injuns air funny critturs," he announced at last, chomping furiously. But Beidler knew, as he watched his famed companion, that he had more than tobacco to chew on. The Crows had given such a burial to Crazy Woman out of respect for Johnson—their greatest enemy, her friend.

Beidler had much to report of Johnson in that spring of 1869. They had come from a winter's work in which only their own strength and skill had kept them alive and won them an income. Now for a few months they would deal with other sorts of white men come into this mountain country—the traders and military men of Fort Hawley, the steamboat captains and their passengers. Such necessary dealings accomplished, however, Johnson had a new sort of score to settle with the Crows.

The trappers reached Johnson's woodyard on the Missouri in an easy day's ride from Crazy Woman's place. As for years now, his dried cordwood stood in piles ready for purchase by river-boat men. Beidler watched, fascinated, while the Crow Killer headed for his bank: the knothole near the top of the gnarled cottonwood stump, just large enough to admit Johnson's hand. Johnson pulled out a roll of bills; and while Beidler unsaddled the horses and staked them out, he counted the money and looked at what was left of his cordwood. Steamboat men had never been known to renege on payment to "wood hawks." No raiding party of Indians had ever burned out the woodyard, or broken into the "bank."

It was some time now during Beidler's stay with Johnson, that Captain Grant Marsh of the Steamer *Nile,* stopping for wood, entertained the two Mountain Men on board. Ice had been obtained from the icehouse at Fort Peck; and to celebrate the Captain's birthday, ice cream was served.[1] The Liver-Eater, ashamed to show his ignorance to the passengers, whispered, "X, whar in hell do this stuff come from?" Just as ignorant, Beidler whispered back, "Shut up, fool; it comes in cans!" Both gulped the "stuff" down.

Beidler had some sort of revenge for such exposure of his and Johnson's innocence. The several ladies on board stared long at the fearsome Mountain Men, and at last one asked Beidler whether he was married. Beidler replied that he was: "To a squaw, ma'am." And where was she now? the enthusiastic passenger asked next. "Sent her to Rome, ma'am." "How wonderful! to Rome, Italy?" was the obvious next question, but Beidler's answer ended the conversation: "No, ma'am, to roam on the prairie."

As he sat combing and hooping scalps by the fire, in their first nights at the woodyard, Beidler watched his partner smoking, looking into the flames. Johnson had something more on his mind than river-boat passengers, and who might look foolish to whom. Nor were his thoughts concerned now with replenishing his wood supply from the vast drift piled up in an eddy just below the camp. Beidler was going on in to Fort Hawley, to sell furs and perhaps the Blackfoot scalps; he

[1] Joseph Mills Hanson, *The Conquest of the Missouri,* pp. 116-19, tells the story in full.

resolved to make a quick trip and get back in time to help finish the woodcutting. But, in fact, "X" would be back in time to help start. For Johnson waited only until Beidler was out of sight, then quickly saddled and mounted his own horse and set off westward. He knew that there was an encampment of Crows somewhere between the mouth of the Musselshell and the Judith River—some of them, likely, the very Crows who had built a cairn for Crazy Woman. With him, as a present, Johnson took a five-gallon keg of whiskey. (According to White-Eye, Johnson thought better of such a gift for young braves; somewhere on his journey he cached the liquor.) After a feud of almost a quarter of a century, the Crow Killer was ready to make peace with the Crows. Braver, more devoted warriors, he knew, had never loosed an arrow. And the body of Crazy Woman had not been left to be torn by wolves.

18 Target for Gray Bear

THE CROW chief Gray Bear, with twenty-six braves, was camped where the Judith empties into the Missouri, east of Fort Benton. On their way back from trapping on the Milk River, north almost into Canada, they were still far from home. Hemmed in by freshets, they were waiting now for the waters to subside before continuing on to Hawley's, where they hoped to sell their peltries. Johnson could have waited and met them at the Fort, but he determined to meet them alone. At the Fort the presence of many others, white and Indian alike, must in itself prevent the active prosecution of their feud. By the Judith, Johnson's and the Crows' own forbearance could be acted out, in formal ending to their years of vendetta.

After a few days by the Judith, the Crows were waiting for

more than a subsiding of rivers. For now Blackfeet swarmed all through that countryside. Though not quarrelsome, the Crows would have been willing enough to take on any one of the several hunting parties of Blackfeet which Gray Bear had already seen. But with Blackfeet roaming in bands all along the Upper Missouri, a mere rifle shot would have served to bring many of them together. The Crows had not labored through a long and bitter winter merely to provide their enemies with these loads of furs. It was a glad day for them when, well along in April, their scouts reported that the Blackfeet had headed south, toward the Yellowstone. Now Gray Bear could give the the long desired command: "We go."

By early afternoon, tepees were struck and fur packs inspected for the miles ahead. After the long spell of gray weather, clouds vanished as if by magic. The sentries were called in. With preparation well under way, Gray Bear walked the fifty yards from camp to a pocket among some scrub trees where he could drink from a cold spring. He scooped water many times in his cupped palms before his thirst was quenched.

Even as he smacked his wet palms on his buckskinned thighs, Gray Bear knew that something was wrong. At the sound of a horse's hoof scraping on the rocks, he swung quickly around. But already the horse had stepped through the brush; its rider sat looking at him. "Do ye know me, Injun?" said Liver-Eating Johnson.

Gray Bear looked at Johnson as if seeing a ghost. ("Fust time I ever seen a red nigger tarn white," the Liver-Eater told White-Eye Anderson years later.) Johnson had his palms out in the universal sign of peace even as Gray Bear half drew his tomahawk; the chief let his weapon slide back into his belt. But though Gray Bear could take his hand off his weapon, his face bore the mark of his fear and his hatred for the man who had killed his tribesmen through so many years. "You are the white hunter who long ago took the trail against us," he replied. "You are the Liver-Eater."

"Right the first whack," said the Crow Killer. "But I've come ter end all thet."

Gray Bear waited for the Killer's explanation.

"Crazy Woman hez a monument," Johnson said. "She wuz buried by Crows."

Gray Bear said that White Badger and his braves had built the old woman's cairn.

"Crow warriors."

Yes, Crow warriors, Gray Bear said, to honor a white woman touched by the Great Spirit. "And to scorn the Blackfeet," he added.

Warmed to his subject, Gray Bear went so far as to invite the old Crow Killer to join his band in an expedition to Big Dry Creek, but this Johnson thought unwise all around. "Too many young bucks with ye," he said wryly. "It war young bucks fust sent me on yer trail." So saying, he gave his mount a sharp slap and rode through the brush, his back a broad target—were it not that he left behind him a friend.

There were exchanges of gifts to be arranged yet with White Badger, the individual Crow chief who had so honored Crazy Woman. But Johnson could count on Gray Bear's passing the word at once, that the Crow Killer desired friendship. In the months ahead, he would even become their brother-in-arms. For just as such an individualist as Liver-Eating Johnson must finally join the forces mustered against frontier-wide Sioux war bands, so too the Crows, after years of indecision, were finally to choose sides. Both must have sympathized with Sioux anger at the coming of so many settlers, and the loss of old hunting grounds. But both, finally, acted to quell uprisings bloody but doomed to failure.

part four

Brother of the Crows

Crow Indians (Absaroka) of the late 1890's

The above print and the other three illustrations facing pages 64, 65 and 80 were all made from rotogravure illustrations in Vol. IV of the multi-volumed set entitled "The North American Indian" written by Edward S. Curtis.

19 White Chief of the Shoshoni

GRAY BEAR and his braves did carry the word that the Crow Killer had buried the hatchet with the Absaroka. News so unexpected spread like wildfire, with diverse speculations and rumors in its wake. Grizzled Mountain Men reserved judgment till all developments might be reported. Fur traders, more cynical, assumed that Johnson's motives were selfish and that the deadly enemy of the Crows, after so many years of open warfare, would now turn to deceit and to murder in secret. Black Elk, a Sioux chief on the Rosebud, tried to turn the news against his Indian enemies. "The livers of the Crows are diseased," he proclaimed. "Eating them has caused Dapiek Absaroka to become as cowardly as the Crows themselves." He went on practically to invite Johnson to sample Sioux livers, or at least the innards of their brothers the Cheyennes, should he wish once again to be strong as the bull buffalo.

Johnson, when he heard the stream of stories coming in to Hawley's, chuckled happily and said he liked people to speculate on his next move. "Ye kin tell ol' Black Elk I mought get his liver next," he told a friendly Cheyenne. Then he saddled, mounted, and rode off toward his Flathead relatives in the Bitter Roots.

Long ago now, some time after securing two Shoshoni scalps from their chief The Fox, Johnson himself had been voted a Shoshoni chief. That circumstance, and Big Anton Sepulveda's desire to see the Liver-Eater before setting out on a trip to California, led to Johnson's next adventure—and Big Anton's last.

Even while Johnson rode toward the Flatheads, Big Anton and Pancho Robles were riding toward him from Apache country. Perhaps a tinge of gray could be seen now in Anton's black beard. His new companion was cousin of that fighter whose place he had taken, the late Apache Joe. Riding together on their powerful Californian horses—Anton's a big black with a white star, Pancho's a three-year-old bay mare from San Luis Obispo—the two men were well-matched in size.

Like Big Anton, Robles wore a heavy black beard and carried rifle, knife, and six-shooters. But Anton had again chosen a companion with virtues and skills complementary to his own. The former *vaquero* who rode beside him now was feared for his Yaqui blood and for the most potent of all his weapons, coiled on the horn of his saddle. This *riata,* made of plaited horsehair no more than a quarter inch in thickness, with a sheen like China silk and the appearance of a child's plaything, was as deadly and as resilient as a live snake. Though its entire seventy-five feet could have been coiled and tucked into a lady's reticule, it had mastered the Sonora grizzly.

The two riders stumbled in on preparations for a fiesta one afternoon, in a small village under the Sangre de Cristo peaks. Children looked wide-eyed at their silver-mounted saddles and bridles. Young men forgot for a moment the evening's dance, on sight of the paired giants and the long knives in their belts. Old men estimated the braided scalps looped through the plaited horsehair. "Español diablo," they muttered to themselves, and bowed respectfully to this warrior whose name they knew, and his companion.

At the far end of the small village street, the two riders came on festivities of special interest to them. Here, in an open space some fifty feet in diameter, many young men were throwing knives at the crudely-drawn heart of a target in the shape of a man. The riders reined in and sat their horses to watch the contestants' prowess. One young man had the best of the competition, for he placed all his throws close to the heart and a few actually inside.

Robles spoke to an old man looking on, and the old man nodded with less evidence of fear than of anticipation. Robles dug out a coin, handed it to the old man, and left to him the necessary commands that the young men stop their throwing. Big Anton, trying till now to catch Robles' eye and call him off from these arrangements, sat still in his saddle and awaited the time for his demonstration of skill.

The old man drew a circle around Robles' coin, then stepped back and motioned the young men too to one side. Big Anton drew his knife and held it a moment in the dancing sunlight for all to see, an Arkansas Toothpick with damascened blade a full sixteen inches in length, point backward and hilt toward the target in the knifeman's huge palm. Now his hand swept back and shot forward, and the knife whipped toward the target and to the exact center of the outlined coin. The old man stepped forward to retrieve the blade, but before he could do so the slender loop of Robles' *riata* noosed the weapon and, answering a flick of Robles' wrist, sent the Bowie sailing into its owner's hand. The whole performance was repeated with machine like precision some dozen times. Finally Anton Sepulveda wiped the blade with the end of his serape, and Robles recoiled his *riata*. Both riders headed off now for the mountains, on their way to find Liver-Eating Johnson, leaving the afternoon's onlookers to their astonishment.

Now while Johnson seldom spoke of his own adventures, he often told of Big Anton Sepulveda's skills and escapades (as he also told of Mariano Modeno's). The whole tale of how Anton picked up fellow Mountain Men on his way north—Arkansas Pete Arnold, Hatchet Jack Ireland, Mad Mose, Mariano, Bear Claw Chris Lapp, Wild Ben, Arapaho Joe—was well worth the telling.

Arkansas Pete had his camp a couple of miles west of the Spanish Peaks. Unlike most trappers, and surely unlike Johnson, Pete wore heavy cavalry boots, no matter what the discomfort in summer. Indeed Pete was sure, on the day when Big Anton came by, that his boots had cost him his life, for he had just now had to take them off. He sat cooling his feet in a small rivulet that ran down from the mountains with just enough murmur to muffle other noises. Pete expected no invaders. He sat talking to himself, as most Mountain Men did, and removing the claws from a fresh grizzly pelt, to save for Bear Claw Chris. His pony, a Comanche mustang, grazed contentedly nearby.

"Shore now, this 'un hez scratched many a tree," was as likely as not the burden of Pete's monologue. "Jist look at them thar claws. Ol' Chris is shorely goin' ter like 'em."

Now he broke off, looked warily about him, and then as if to answer himself began again: "It's a good thing, though, that I got in a good shot, or ol' Arkansas would be cold meat now. My, *whut* a rake this b'ar could give a feller."

Pete looked at his pony, which had one ear cocked. The pony looked back at him. Pete wiggled his toes in the cool water, shrugged against his sun-baked shirt, and thought to look around him once more. But a pebble fell somewhere behind him, and the pony shied. Clearly, Pete was ambushed. Yet now he could not move. Though his rifle lay next to his hand, no enemy would let him raise the weapon or even look around. "Whoever's thar, come on up," said Arkansas Pete.

He heard a low rumbling chuckle, then a loud laugh, and "I will give you three times to guess who is here, Señor." Pete began to pull on his boots coolly and methodically, without glancing around. "One's 'nuff," he said. "Ye air Big Anton, an' ye hez got a Mexican Greaser wi' ye."

Where the Rio Dolores, or River of Sorrow, joins the Rio Colorado in southeastern Utah, the La Sal Mountains were long a favored meeting place of Mountain Men; though the Utes who held this land were exceptionally warlike, they allowed the Mountain Men free passage to the La Sal range, in a sort of unwritten agreement among free fighting men. Riding west and north, in search of companions, Big Anton Sepulveda and Pancho Robles and Arkansas Pete Arnold found the La Sal camping ground just as four trappers there were striking tents: Hatchet Jack, Mad Mose, Mariano, and—"Great Jehosophat, Pocahontas, an' John Smith, if'n it ain't Big Anton!"—old Bear Claw.

"Whar's Joe?" Bear Claw demanded.

Anton dismounted and lifted the old man to his feet in a bear hug. "José was killed by the Apaches, old *compañero*. Twenty-six of them, including two chiefs, have since followed him."

"An' I know thet's so, Anton," the old man said—so, if Big Anton said so. He turned now, quickly, to greet Arkansas Pete.

That night, while the flames of the campfire leaped to canyon walls, it was agreed that with trapping season still months ahead, all seven Mountain Men should ride together to see the Crow Killer. Jack and Mariano were posted to take turns on guard till morning, but there were hours of talk for these lonely, talk-hungry men before any of them settled down to sleep. Talk of recent deaths among Mountain Men—of Lobo Ned, burned alive at the stake by the Cheyennes. Talk of Mountain Men who took vengeance on their friends' killers —of Mormon Jake, who, Bear Claw said, "drunk ther red coons' blood," of Old Hatcher and the way he "gagged 'em and tied 'em in trees, head down," and above all of Liver-Eating Johnson, the Crow Killer. Talk finally from Mad Mose, whose life work had been not trapping but simply the killing of Indians (and who, his six hearers believed, had no memory of any time before his own scalping). Mose had taken on himself the avenging of Lobo Ned.

"I follered them Cheyennes fer a week," Mose said, "an' caught up wi' 'em on Laramie Plain. I caught 'em asleep an' kilt the two guards wi' my hatchet. Then I stabbed sixteen in the guts, skelped 'em all, an' chopped off their arms." He relived the bloody scene with mounting excitement. "I leff 'em runnin' aroun' in circles, wisht now I'd a-burned 'em."

"Naw, leave 'em live," cried Hatchet Jack. "I useter kill 'em an' *then* cut 'em up, now I chops 'em ter pieces an' hopes they'll live."

As the morning sun topped the La Sals, the seven Mountain Men rode northward through the rough, wild country of the Sheberetch and Yampa Utes. Skirting the Uintahs, they rode through Johnson's old hunting grounds and on into the Wasatch range. Now once again they picked up recruits: Wild Ben at his summer camp on Weber River, and Arapaho Joe after they crossed Bear River and hit the trail to Fort Hall.

Bear Claw was riding advance as the nine Mountain Men headed on north along the banks of the Blackfoot. By all appearance, the old man had eyes only for the matched sets of bear claws just presented him by Wild Ben, fine specimens so long polished that they seemed jewels. But Chris had his mind on the horizon as well. When he reined in, the others knew he had spotted potential trouble and rode up to him at a fast canter. Following his gesture, they saw a lone Indian rider on a small promontory to the left of the trail. The Indian beckoned, alternately throwing out his hands in sign of friendship. "Shoshoni," Hatchet Jack said, and he rode toward the Indian, loosening his favorite weapon. The others followed at a distance, covering Jack with their rifles.

Hatchet Jack prided himself on his knowledge of Indian tongues. When he rejoined his companions he knew of a going war between tribes, and had pretty well conceived what adventurous part therein the Mountain Men could play. "Thet's Wahni's son," he said, "thet Hatcher saved from the big cat. He says the Nez Perce hez killed Shoshoni women and children, out gatherin' roots on the prairie. He says they's sneaked up an' killed Wahni an' some of his braves. He says he wants Liver-Eatin's help, thought mebbe Liver-Eatin' was with us."

Bear Claw remarked that perhaps the nine Mountain Men

could now recruit Johnson, to fight along with them against the Nez Perces, since he had been Wahni's friend.

"Liver-Eatin' kain't hardly pass this 'un up," Jack said. "This Injun here says, Liver-Eatin' wuz voted a chief of ther Shoshoni ten y'ars back." As chief, his friends knew, Johnson would be honor bound to take up this Shoshoni fight.

There was some astonishment expressed among the Mountain Men that "we'd be a-helpin' Diggers," and Pancho Robles began to see Big Anton's trip to California postponed indefinitely, but their action was at once resolved. Rollicking along, they crossed the plains of the Snake River and entered the foothills of the Bitter Roots. Along their way they fell in with twenty trappers from the Uintahs, who set aside all business plans in favor of an Indian fight. They could count, too, on finding perhaps a dozen more Mountain Men trading for horses with the Flatheads. The force they could present to Liver-Eating Johnson, to aid him in avenging "his" Shoshonis on an expedition he had not at all anticipated, would come to some forty Mountain Men besides Johnson himself and Del Gue.

But in fact more than Mountain Men wanted to fight beside Liver-Eating Johnson, against the Nez Perces. Young Wahni brought twenty-eight excellent braves from his small Shoshoni village. Fifty Flatheads volunteered. The Crow chief Big Antelope, in climax to the recruiting, offered his people's old enemy his entire band of thirty warriors.

Johnson accepted: "Guess I got me an army!" He had one hundred and fifty to command, against an enemy he knew next to nothing about. Some of his Mountain Men, in their indiscriminate scorn for all Indians, would as soon have turned on their Flathead hosts or on their other Indian allies. Johnson himself, though he had long respected Crow and Flathead and Shoshoni, took for granted that they were going to fight against despised "Diggers." Like Mariano Modeno, he thought that "all *Indios* between the mountains and the sea are lizards who live in the earth and eat grasses." Bear Claw had to warn him that the division of the Nez Perces which they were setting out to fight (the Salmon Eaters) were not to be scorned. "Nez Perce no good a-fightin' on ther ground," he generalized. "But these varmints we're a-goin' after is ther kind thet rides hosses."

The readying of gear for the expedition to Nez Perce country proceeded largely without incident. Arkansas Pete, jealous perhaps that Wild Ben had got in before him with a present of bear claws to Bear Claw, did choose these days for an around-the-clock polishing of his own set and then a formal presentation: "I seen them claws thet young feller give ye, Chris. They wuz frum ol' b'ars, wi' ther points wore off. Hyar is a set from a young b'ar I kilt specially." And Pete was rewarded by Bear Claw's most resounding "Jehosophat."

Now and then more volunteers came in, white and Indian, including three Utes renowned as trackers. Johnson accepted their offer of help, though he assigned to Arkansas Pete and Mariano Modeno the special assignment, "Watch them Utes." Pete and Mariano nodded gladly.

The eighth day after Big Anton's party came in from the south, the expedition got under way. The hundred-and-sixty-odd fighting men spread out in groups. The Utes rode ahead, but with Mariano or Pete ever following close. Each party of Indians rode as a body, distinct from other tribes. Only the Mountain Men rode out of formation, singly sometimes, or in twos and threes, or even mixed with whatever group of Indians they might want to look in on.

At night there were five separate campfires. Now Mariano took over almost entirely the watch over the Utes' comings and goings. It was soon the Mountain Men's joke that none of them had ever seen Mariano sleep. Long after guards were posted and most of the trappers bedded down, his lithe figure darted between firelight and outlying darkness. Come morning, his flashing black eyes seemed to have observed all the night's developments. Come evening once again, after the day's hard ride, he squatted like an Indian, listening for a while perhaps to the other trappers' exchange of tales, but forever on the prowl, forever whetting the long, keen blade of his scalping knife, once broad and heavy but now narrow and wisp-thin. No man unless Mariano himself knew how many throats it had severed, or how many scalps it had taken, for Mariano kept no notches. His beautiful Hawken rifle, too, Mariano kept in perfect condition (and indeed it was such a piece that, bequeathed to General A. H. Jones and handed down in his family, it still repays fond care). But the knife was Mariano's love: "El solución," he called it. Each night, when Pete's cherished cavalry boots were off and their owner safely asleep, Mariano honed his blade on their soft top-leather.

Traveling south and west, the Shoshoni's avengers crossed the Lemhi River into the rough country bordering on the Nez Perces' lands. Whites and Indians alike put out videttes, in addition to the Utes who still rode ahead. After they crossed the middle fork of the Salmon, Wahni described (from his scouts' reports) the foe's position. Now Johnson sent the three Utes far ahead to reconnoiter round the main Nez Perce encampment, on the east side of the Weiser.

Perhaps he had not mistrusted them enough, nor realized in full their capacity for trickery. Nor would Johnson himself, so skilled in directing his own course away from ambush, prove equally skilled in choosing a safe course for an entire command. The Mountain Men and their Crow and Flathead and Shoshoni allies rode on slowly toward the meeting place prearranged with the Utes.

Next day, when the sun was straight overhead, the leader of the three Utes returned to announce that the unwarned village lay open to attack. He then rode abruptly away at right angles from the expedition's course, and signaled that all should follow into the mouth of a wide canyon. Johnson raced ahead of his fighting men, let them ride on for a time, but soon held up his hand for a halt. Apparently he mistrusted the lay of the land, or perhaps the Ute's headlong dash into unscouted terrain. He

raised in his stirrups to sniff at the slight breeze coming out of
the canyon's mouth.

Suddenly he shouted warning, "This air a trap!" and he reined
his own horse behind a boulder. At once the mouth of the canyon
and the approach along both sides erupted in a terrific fusillade.
None of the Mountain Men needed to be told what they were
up against: Their foe was armed with Spencer repeating rifles.
Only their own constant, instinctive awareness of nearest shelter saved them now. Only their skill as individual fighting men
saved them from Johnson's failures in tactics. At that, one bullet
in that first fusillade went through Mad Mose's chest. One Flathead brave and three of the twenty-eight Shoshoni were killed
on their horses, and several others were wounded on their way
to cover. But the bulk of Johnson's party did find hiding place in
the rocks. And when the main body of Nez Perces, splendidly
mounted on their war ponies, thundered out of the canyon, they
were met by a withering return fire. They too had miscalculated.
Cut down almost at once, themselves the ambushed, they left
to their tribesmen stationed at the canyon's mouth only the task
of killing what invaders they could before their own certain
deaths.

Perhaps in the general confusion Big Anton Sepulveda did
not realize where the greater danger now lay. In any event, he
stood to shoot at the last of the mounted Nez Perces. But as fire
belched from his six-shooters, a Nez Perce behind a rock to
the left of him took quick aim; Big Anton stumbled and fell
heavily. Pancho Robles, still on his mount as became a *Califor-
nio,* surged from where, behind a big boulder, he too had been
firing. Dropping both pistols, he seized his *riata.* The loop snaked
out through the gunsmoke and settled over the head of the Nez
Perce who had shot his comrade. Quickly snubbing the braid on
the high horn of his saddle, he spoke to his horse, and the highly
trained animal swerved. The Nez Perce was dragged almost from
behind his rock before, suddenly, the quarter-inch loop cut
through his neck. There was no use in Pancho's snapping the

Indian's head to Big Anton, for Big Anton was dead. Instead, he sent it rolling over the rocks to Liver-Eating Johnson. The gift came handy.

For Johnson had emptied his rifle and six-shooters and had only his Bowie with which to meet one oncoming Indian still on horseback. Reaching quickly, he seized the gruesome object which rolled toward him and hurled it at his live foe. The two heads smashed together; the mounted Nez Perce pitched to the ground. Now Johnson rushed out with his knife. From behind the rocks Mountain Men and Indians raced toward the canyon's mouth. Seizing riderless horses, the warriors of three tribes mounted to pursue what few surviving Nez Perces fled.

When Johnson and his comrades began the tally of the dead on both sides, they could not find Mariano and Pete—their Ute-watchers. Johnson felt some concern that, ahead with the Utes, they might have fallen into the ambush prepared for all. But soon enough Del Gue pointed down the canyon to where they came. The leader of the Utes rode freely between them, but with Mariano's six-shooter pointed steadily toward him. As the three rode close, Johnson could see that the Ute's face was covered with blood. From time to time Arkansas Pete slapped him with the fresh scalps of his tribesmen.

"Para el capitán," said Mariano as he forced the Ute to ride before Johnson.

"Saved him fer ye, Liver-Eatin'," cried Pete in high good humor.

Johnson took one great step, grasped the captive, and threw him to the ground. The Ute sprang at once to his feet, his face scowling black hatred.

The trappers gathered round, each with his own advice as to how best a renegade might be disposed of. Arkansas Pete slapped him once again with the hardening pair of scalps. The Ute quivered with his contempt for those who would bait him thus unarmed.

"Traitor," Johnson said, and he waved back the ring of Mountain Men and Indians. "Traitor, me an' ye is a-goin' ter hug. Throw him yer knife, Mariano." Johnson himself stood empty-handed, his own knife untouched in his belt.

The Ute, powerfully built, eager to kill even one of his foes, caught Mariano's knife as it sailed through the air. His one darting movement became a leap toward Johnson. But Johnson's moccasined foot caught his wrist and sent the weapon flying; Johnson's fist struck him, as he stood astonished, between the eyes. He fell heavily, but in an instant he was back on his feet.

Once again he caught the blade that Mariano sent whirling back to him. Once again he sprang forward, this time for an upward slash. But—blinded perhaps by rage at having even once been disarmed by an adversary using no weapon—he held the knife low too soon. Even as his weapon cleaved mightily upward, the Crow Killer, throwing himself to one side, at the same time brought up his foot with a kick that lifted the Ute two feet in the air. Still agile, the Ute whirled but only to take another kick beneath the chin. His teeth were driven together; he fell flat and nerveless on his back. Stepping over him, Johnson took the blade from his hand and swiftly scalped him. But he would allow no more play with a still living, suffering Indian. He returned the knife to Mariano, and at once Mariano cut the Ute's throat. "One more fer Mad Mose," Johnson said.

Mariano turned next to the merciful killing of the Nez Perce wounded, already scalped by the Shoshoni. Johnson went to the dead body of Big Anton. "Slickest hand whut ever throwed a sticker," he told Pancho Robles, seated there. Next he went to where Hatchet Jack, instead of chopping his dead foes' flesh as was his custom, sat by his dead friend Mad Mose.

Mose lay where he had fallen, among the rocks. His matted beard was full of blood coughed from his chest wound. Surely, it seemed, he must have been dead before he fell from his horse, yet even now he seemed to be trying to roll over, trying to scramble to his feet, trying to rise; and his hatchet was still in hand. Only the naked spot on the top of his head, where he had been scalped long ago by a Blackfoot tomahawk, proved by its lack of beating pulse that Mose was dead indeed. Hatchet Jack had brushed the gray hair back from the old man's eyes, and he fanned away the desert gnats.

"Many's ther red nigger we hounded off this airth tergether," Jack cried.

"We knows thet, Jack," said the Crow Killer.

"He war like a father ter me."

Johnson seemed to speak once more, then cleared his throat and turned away.

"Come on now, Liver-Eater," Del Gue urged. "No use ter keep his sicrit now. Tell Jack who Mose war."

And Johnson turned and looked once more at his dead friend. "He war John Morgan," he said at last, "husband ter Crazy Woman on the Musselshell."

None of Johnson's hearers thought to ask how he had known, or whether he had confirmation from Mad Mose: If Johnson spoke thus, positively, he knew. Nor did any of them ask why he had kept such a secret: Mad, John Morgan and his wife could be of little comfort to one another; and if perhaps sometimes sane, John Morgan must be let to decide for himself what life he should lead after his family's disaster.

But the Mountain Men did demand that Johnson tell "Mose" Morgan's story, even that part of it which they most of them knew. So Johnson did tell once more of the Morgans' camping for wagon repairs and some rest by the Musselshell. Perhaps it seemed to some of them, now for the first time, that the Liver-Eater knew more details of the Morgans' story, through their weeks of peace there and their one afternoon of horror, than he could likely have learned from Crazy Woman. Now he told how John Morgan, bound and scalped and slashed and carried away by the Blackfeet after they had killed his children, escaped in his first night of captivity and then roamed the mountains, demented. "He's been wi' Jack hyar most o' ther time since," Johnson concluded. "I knowed Jack would tek care o' him."

"Bless ye, Liver-Eater," said the hatchet man, "bless yer heart."

The Mountain Men buried Big Anton and Mad Mose on their last battlefield; the Flatheads, Crows, and Shoshoni tied their few dead to the backs of Nez Perce ponies for the long ride home.

One green young trapper from the Yellowstone drew laughs from Mountain Men and Indians alike by asking, "Ain't we a-goin' ter bury these Injuns?" He meant the sixty-three Nez Perce warriors whose bodies were piled together.

"No need, young *hombre,*" Mariano Modeno answered him, and Mariano pointed to where, in the vast blue sky, specks sailed warily in wide circles. Observing his victim's repressed shudder, Mariano went on for the benefit of all his audience: "I was too hasty. I should have let the birds at them before they died."

20 Biscuits for Blackfeet

FORT McPHERSON, Nebraska, in the summer of 1871, was the generally announced meeting place for Mountain Men, and any plainsmen, Indians, soldiers, and wolfers who might want to join in with the Mountain Men's plans. Liver-Eating Johnson went to McPherson, on the big black that had been Big Anton's, to get up a small party for a trapping trip into the Big Horn Mountains. So, to the general amusement, did "Buffalo Bill" Cody attend the McPherson gathering. Young "White-

Eye Jack" Anderson, meeting both men for the first time, aimed to join in with just such a man as Johnson—and has reported what supreme contempt Johnson had for Cody.

"Buffalo Bill" accomplished his purpose at McPherson, even though (as Doc Carver, the originator of his show, has stated) "no western man ever took him seriously . . . he was considered by every westerner to be the poorest shot on the plains . . . he never killed an Indian in his life." [1] The very model of buckskin fashion, Cody recruited the actors he needed for a play, of which he was to be the hero, in Eastern theatres.

Johnson too succeeded in his more modest recruiting. Pete Coyle had already promised Del Gue that he would make a third, and he recommended "White-Eye" to complete the party. Johnson looked the young fellow over and shook hands. It was agreed that they should first go to Fort Pierre, on the Missouri, where Pete had left his equipment, and thence strike due west to the mountains. After buying such supplies as they needed from the sutler's, the four partners mounted their horses one hot morning in July and set out for Dakota. Del Gue, whether in joke or in innocent admiration, suggested even as they headed up the Platte, "Liver-Eatin', whyn't ye ask Buffalo Bill along?"

"Mought git his britches dirty in them Big Horns," Johnson said.

"White-Eye" could always tell a good story, as is proved by those reminiscences on which so much in these pages has been based. His tales must have been a welcome addition to the campfire lore on the trek to Wyoming. He must, surely, have rehearsed more than once the tale of his own "white eye" or, rather, snow-white eyebrow: his escape with Yankee Judd from a Sioux war party, the gale at their backs, the prairie set afire, his and Judd's exhausted horses; their dismounting at a buffalo wallow and their self-immersion in a foot of water; their long

[1] Letter from Carver to R. W. T. dated Tampa, Florida, February 16, 1927.

wait in the wallow till the war party passed over the burned-out prairie in pursuit of their riderless horses; the burning buffalo chip that struck Jack in the eye and on the eyebrow; his and Judd's weary flight to the camp of the famed friendly chief, Whistler.

Johnson and his partners met no enemy now, though their route ran directly through the Black Hills of the Sioux. Del Gue, assuring White-Eye that "Whar Liver-Eatin' goes, they's bound ter be trouble," argued the theory that if no Sioux fell upon them Johnson was merely saving the party for a fight with the Blackfeet. Pete Coyle, as to dispute Del's theory, reminisced that once "way back" he had known Johnson to go a whole season "wi'out no Injuns showin' up." Johnson, finally appealed to as he sat smoking by the fire, would announce only, "If'n thar's any tenderfoots hyar thet's feared o' Injuns, they'd best stay out o' ther Big Horns."

Any mistrust which White-Eye may have felt was surely aroused when he first saw Johnson's cabin. The cabin was set directly over a spring, some fifty feet above the bottom of a canyon. But the canyon was blind. And White-Eye, though his short apprenticeship had already taken him into a great deal of action, nevertheless had a preference for open plains where he could not be boxed. "There's only one way out o' this pocket," he told Del and Pete.

But neither would give him satisfactory answer. "I allus tol' ther Liver-Eater this wuz a trap," Del said, with a far from reassuring pat on the back. "S'posen ther Injuns hez already spotted us?" he asked Pete.

"Then we'll have ter climb this mounting," Pete said—and pointed vaguely toward sheer cliffsides rearing fifteen hundred feet straight up.

Pressed further by White-Eye, Pete would suggest only the general explanation that if the cabin had no escape, Johnson must have planned that it should have none, and that he baited the Indians in any way he could. White-Eye urged that at least the three partners could ask Johnson why they were situated so, but Pete and Del solemnly assured him that they must not.

In the month they had before the snows came, the four partners had ample time to work out their respective chores. It was settled that each, in his turn, would stay by the cabin to watch the saddle horses and their pack animals, three big Missouri mules. As boss of the outfit, Johnson delegated the skinning chore to the others, smoking his pipe while their work went on. The trappers learned soon that they were in a real "fur pocket," amidst plentiful mink and beaver. The skinning sessions, in the cabin at night, would surely have seemed tedious indeed without the exchange of stories.

Those night sessions were a revelation to White-Eye. Given that rarity, an eager new audience, Del and Pete expounded the lore of the mountains hours on end. Even the Crow Killer, sitting in his dark corner back of the fireplace, smoking his pipe and stroking his great beard, broke in from time to time to set the record straight. These men spoke of hair-raising adventures and dreadful deaths as if they were commonplace. They filled in to the last detail the stories of bloody engagements which were legend to the plainsman but in which they themselves had taken part.

One cloudy night as the others sat skinning out the pelts, Johnson suddenly rose and went outside, as always with his rifle. When he returned an hour later, covered with the heavy flakes of the first snowfall, he stood his heavy rifle in the corner and sat down again in his usual corner. "Hosses an' mules air gone," he said after a time, and filled and lighted his pipe.

"Wa'al now, I tol' ye, Pete," said Del Gue, slamming a half-skinned-out pelt to the dirt floor and getting to his feet. "I tol' ye wharever Liver-Eatin' goes, thar's Injuns."

Johnson chuckled and puffed out smoke.

"A'right, ye told us," White-Eye said—or so, at least, he made himself out as saying, in his later tales—"but what'll we do now? We're shut in, wi' no way out. We've lost hosses, pelts, ever'thin'!"

Del Gue, instead of answering, opened the door. The blast of wind that entered sent snow all over the room. "Whew," he said, "thar'll be three feet o' thet in ther mornin'."

Johnson knocked out his pipe on the stone fireplace and got to his feet. Like a Viking giant he stood, with the fire playing on his red beard; White-Eye wasn't sure whether the parting was grin or snarl. He looked now at the young trapper directly but spoke to Del. "Del," he said, "I lost more'n all o'ye, didn't I?"

"Yas," Del said, "ye lost ther best hoss in all o' ther West." And such indeed was the reputation of the big black with the white star, that had been Big Anton's.

"Don't ye fret then, young 'un," Johnson said, "we'll git out o' hyar an' we won't be follered."

Even Del Gue looked at Johnson in surprise. Surely they could not leave the canyon as they had come in, for any foe would be on constant lookout from now on. "Blackfoots?" he asked.

Johnson nodded. "Biggest biscuit eaters in this worl'," he said. And unbelievably, he built up a roaring fire, "ter fool them Blackfoots," he said—and stood in front of it.

Pete Coyle spoke up: "It must be midnight, Liver-Eatin'; we'd better be skedaddlin'."

"One more chore 'fore we go," said Johnson, "one more chore fer Crazy Woman." White-Eye was never to be quite sure whether Johnson had wanted the Blackfeet to break in on their winter's trapping, or whether his elaborate plans had been made only for the possibility. He took two bread pans from the wall and dumped a large measure of flour in each. Next he took a large can from the rude shelf, dumped perhaps half its contents into the flour, and mixed thoroughly before calling to Del for water.

"What's he a-doin'?" White-Eye asked Del, as Johnson began to mix the dough.

"Makin' biscuits," replied Del, and then added—as if only in slow realization that White-Eye's question might not be so stupid as it sounded—"Liver-Eatin' makes ther best biscuits in ther mountings. Guess he thinks them Blackfoots is a-goin' ter be hungry."

The young trapper summoned up his own dead-pan humor. "I've made biscuits some," he said, "and I'd say he puts in too much bakin' powder."

Johnson turned and directed at White-Eye that gaze which had caused so many men to shrink. "This ain't bakin' powder," he said.

Now at last Pete Coyle guffawed, slapping White-Eye on the back. "Thet's wolfer's strychnine, young 'un," he said. "Bakin' powder biscuits air fer whites. These kind air special made fer nice Blackfoot Injuns."

Soon Johnson had his biscuits formed and placed in the bear-grease-smeared pans. "Thar's a-goin' ter be some spiled livers around hyar," said Del Gue. The pans smoked, and the biscuits browned.

Shortly after midnight, Johnson unbarred the heavy rear door —which, so far as White-Eye till then knew, simply led to some cache of supplies up against the cliff. "Built this cabin fer some such time ez this," Johnson said, stepped outside, and was gone for a whole half-hour. When he returned, he said, "She's cl'ared up, an' ther stars air a-shinin'. We mought as well shake out through ther tunnel." He placed a slow-burning hardwood log on the fire. He set the two pans of brown, delectable biscuits in front where they would hold their warmth.

Now not even Del could wait. "Ye really dug a tunnel through hyar, Liver-Eatin'?" he demanded.

"Not dug, it's nat'ral."

"Right out o' this canyon?"

Johnson nodded.

White-Eye still looked doubtful of what he might be in for, and Johnson condescended to elaborate: The tunnel would take them to ten feet above the floor of another canyon. "Jist a leetle drop," he said in high good humor, as if only that were his young partner's concern.

"Never seed Liver-Eatin' so cheerful," said Del to White-Eye.

The trappers' further preparations must be simple. They knew they were in for no picnic, even after escaping the Blackfeet. They must walk the long two hundred and fifty miles to Laramie—torture for men accustomed to riding horseback. They could at least be sure that after they left the other end of the tunnel, the falling snow would cover their tracks before any pursuers might break through the back door. But once the snow stopped they must travel by night and hide, with constant lookouts, during the day.

They inspected their weapons and inserted fresh loads. They honed their knives and hatchets. Johnson surveyed the room thoughtfully. Observing now what some shrewd foe might see as suspicious, he dumped the remainder of the strychnine into the kettle of flour and threw the emptied can out the door. He looked last and lovingly at his biscuits, "set so nat'ral" by the fire. "They'll think we wuz skeart off jist as we wuz about to eat," he said. Chuckling, he motioned for the others to follow him into the tunnel. There he closed and barred the door once again, from the outside.

Apparently Johnson never went back to reckon his score with the Blackfeet. He was pulling out from many favorite haunts now, and taking little or no trouble to preserve cabins and rude furnishings which had been his. White-Eye, though, heard the rest of the story from Old Jim Baker, survivor of the days when Sublette and Hugh Glass roamed the mountains.

"I war wi' 'Rapaho Joe in ther Big Horns thet spring," said Old Jim. "We went up thet canyon jist as ther snow wuz a-meltin' an' flushed ther buzards off ther skeletons o' twenty-nine red coons. They wuz a-layin' all o' them along ther canyon wall, es if they wuz a-tryin' ter climb it."

"Could ye tell the tribes?" asked White-Eye.

"Wa'al shore," said Old Jim a little testily. "They wuz Blackfoots, er I don't know a Blackfoot nigger when I see one."

21 A Last Departure

DEL GUE WAS tired after the adventure in the Big Horns, and told his partner that he wanted to hunt and fish and above all to stay away from Indians. Johnson, sympathetically, suggested that they repair to the cabin on the Little Snake which he had taken over so long ago from Old Hatcher. The partners arrived in the fall of 1872 and set to making the place habitable once again. They rebuilt the old corral and gathered some horse feed and plenty of wood for the fireplace. Then, while Del determinedly set to his hunting and fishing, Johnson put out a line of traps. He knew his partner, and his traps had not been out for a week before Del stated his desire to "come in on ther deal." Even so, the winter was easy for both old Mountain Men. They trapped till the big snows came, without any adventure worthy of mention, then spent the rest of the months till spring sitting peaceably by their fireside.

Lazing those months away, the partners decided they would like to see Mariano Modeno again, at his home camp on the Big Thompson. So when snows melted and grasses grew, they prepared again to travel. Del had some sense that Johnson's preparations were unusually careful, but he was astonished, on the clear May morning when they packed, to see his partner take everything from the cabin except the rude furniture. He was the more astonished when Johnson packed dry fodder against the walls of the cabin.

"I'll never need this roost no more," the Crow Killer said,

and touched a match to the fodder. But it was not Johnson's way, it was not the Mountain Men's way, simply to destroy what might be another man's shelter for a season of trapping or in a season of need. Only this cabin where he had once left The Swan, did he destroy. A brisk breeze from the north fanned the flames; they leaped and danced around the walls of Hatcher's ancient "roost."

With their three pack horses loaded, the partners mounted their saddle horses and set off, Johnson with the packreins in one hand. Down the valley they rode, but after a few minutes Johnson left the trail, riding ahead of Del among the rocks. They halted as they came to a large cairn, square-cornered, its top stones bedded in with dirt to show that they had lain untouched for years. The Crow Killer spat through his beard.

Then, as the sun shone through a cleft in the rocks above them, a beam struck the top of Johnson's sepulchre squarely in its center, to light up the huge rattlesnake which lay there, fresh from its hibernation. The tail of the reptile whirred now, incessantly; the beady eyes were fastened on the trappers; the long forked tongue leaped out at them.

Del brought his rifle to his shoulder and lined up his sights perfectly, but Johnson's big hand knocked the gun aside. "Leave ther crittur be, Del," he said, with what was perhaps intended for a grin, "it'll mek a good watchdog fer me." He turned his horse back onto the trail.

Riding behind, Del knew that he had seen what only two men had ever before observed—Johnson himself, and the Indian who a full generation ago had spread Johnson's secret. Before they came to the bend in the canyon, he had time to look back just once toward the blazing cabin on the banks of the Little Snake. Del Gue was a rough, untutored Mountain Man but one easily impressed. The sense he had now was of a wind sweeping down out of the Wind River Mountains to obliterate a landmark in the history of the West.

22 Mariano and the Ute Chief

MARIANO MODENO was small, but tough as an oak. Educated, he said, by priests, he spoke thirteen Old World languages, could read five more, and to these had added the linguistics of a dozen Indian tribes. His friends managed not to regard him as a "Mexican" despite his birth in Taos and his three-fourths Spanish blood and his one-fourth Indian. After all, he had been a Mountain Man now since the early 1830's; he had learned his trade with such giants as Sublette, Hugh Glass, and Bill Williams. He felt an unqualified, never-explained hatred for all Indians. He gave homage to one man only, Liver-Eating Johnson.

Sometimes it seemed if not to Johnson at least to Del Gue that even such a friend as Mariano could be unnecessarily cruel to his foe. As example, take his treatment of Captain Jack, the Ute chief.

Now like Johnson, Mariano Modeno married a Flathead girl, though their methods of winning their wives were quite unlike. Mariano bought one Marie (from the French trapper who had stolen her and two other girls in a raid) and renamed her John. As John, she covered the trapping trails with Mariano beside her for years, and herself killed many Indians. At last Mariano built John a house but at the same time set her up in business, in the Big Thompson valley of Colorado. By the large log house, built with the help of other trappers and furnished from Santa Fe and Taos, stood a dormitory-fort, defended always by what wandering Mountain Men might be taking advantage of Mariano's hospitality.

The valley of the Big Thompson was beautiful country, and years earlier Mariano had promised himself he would build there. But the site had another advantage: Here he could build a toll bridge at the ford, on the main emigrant trail from Arkansas to the Pacific. Mariano's fort, which he named Namaqua, became a stage station on the Overland Stage Route in 1862. He hired old friends from Taos to man the business but gave over-all charge to John, his Indian wife.

Mariano would lead no home life himself. To him, "home" was a replenishing point for powder and ball or, infrequently, for a homecooked meal. Mariano was careful of his reputation for never resting, just as he cherished his fame among the trappers as one "too danged small to hit." In fact, of course, Mariano slept; at least, he once let Johnson and Del Gue see him bed down. And in fact, his tough hide was full of Indian lead. Once General A. H. Jones (according to his son's tale in 1932), walking with Mariano, asked his permission to touch an astonishing lump in his flesh. With Mariano's grinning permission, the General did touch or, rather, press the lump, and out popped a heavy caliber bullet. "That is Arapaho lead I have carried twenty years," said Mariano; "there are a lot working out of my hide lately."

Mariano's appearance now in his fifties is astonishingly described in material variously published in 1890. Though the details in the many "reminiscences" differed (Mariano appearing in one, for example, as a Frenchman), they all clearly have the same source.

"Nearly thirty years ago," one of the accounts begins,[1] "when traveling in the Taos Valley of New Mexico, we chanced to camp for the night at the same watering place with a dude-looking Spaniard named Mariano Modeno. He had a squaw wife who wore a blanket and moccasins. Mariano, himself, wore a blanket coat which was gaily ornamented with silk. . . ." It is our good luck, indeed, that Mariano on this occasion was traveling with full retinue: "He traveled in a dilapidated carriage with a pair of Hawken rifles in easy reach. His team of four

[1] *Field and Farm*, IX, no. 13 (March 29, 1890).

horses was guided by an Indian, who rode the right-wheeler and directed the leaders with a jerk-line."

But the writer made no pretense to have seen Mariano's home, or his estate "well-fixed with cattle, sheep and horses." Del Gue could have testified to the impression these could make. Rounding a bend in a trail through towering trees, in what had seemed primeval country, Del's mouth hung open in astonishment. Here were cleared acres in which no stump was to be seen. Here were not only fort, toll bridge, and house, but a large vegetable garden, horse corrals, a huge barn filled high with feed, a stockade for oxen, an enclosure with four milk cows, a chicken yard in which hens scratched industriously. . . .

"Mariano buys most of thet stuff," Johnson told him, "from emigrants passin'." But the wonder explained was a wonder still.

The partners found Mariano in a large rocker, apparently mending the riding equipment stacked all around him. His black hair hung down over his face. He wore only one garment, frayed linsey-woolsey trousers. Rubbing at something held across his knee with a smooth stone, he looked anything but the proud Indian fighter.

"Polishin' harness," whispered Johnson to Del.

The partners rode right up to the porch before Mariano raised his head. Only then, as Mariano stood up, did Johnson see what the foremost Indian killer of Colorado was working at. Mariano held up for their inspection a Ute scalp—a fresh Ute scalp.

Now later storytellers, like those who wrote their reminiscences of Mariano in 1890, reported that Mariano and Captain Jack divided the West romantically between them—that "on this certain occasion Modeno was down in New Mexico simply to allow Jack to have northern Colorado to himself." But in fact Jack— that pariah and traitor to his own tribe—had promised Mariano a death at the burning stake; Mariano had promised Jack "the limb." Already, in their hundred-odd battles, Mariano had killed most of Jack's original band; fifty scalps on two walls told the story.

Fired now by Johnson's and Del's arrival, Mariano at once offered to take them on a hunt for Captain Jack and "two or three more Ute outlaws" recently joined with him—"at least one for each of us." Del, according to his own story, would as soon have forgotten Indians for a time. But Johnson—especially after a few nights' sleep on blankets spread on a floor—was anxious to get on the trail. (There were, of course, beds enough in Mariano's house, but he himself preferred the porch.) Johnson figured that a week's expedition should surely fetch in Jack's scalp. But for once he underestimated a foe's cunning. In three separate ambuscades, ranging out a hundred miles all over that northern Colorado country, Johnson did manage to kill and scalp two of Jack's braves, but the chief himself escaped. Finally, at the end of the summer, Mariano took the trail alone against his old enemy, after securing his friends' promise that they would remain till he returned.

The days passed, and the weeks, and Mariano did not return. Johnson wanted to take the trail northward by early fall, but he could not leave. Finally one evening, after more than three weeks, Johnson told Del that if one more day passed and Mariano had not returned, they must go after him.

"Mebbe thet Ute got him," suggested Del.

"No red coon ever lived, could salt away thet Spaniard," said Johnson. "But he mought hev broke a leg."

Del kept his own counsel.

The next day they spent fishing, frying up the mess of trout they caught, and talking over the winter's trapping prospects with three wolfers up from Gunnison. This last of the days Johnson figured they could wait for Mariano passed quietly till, just at sunset, the dogs belonging to one of the wolfers set up a clamor. Johnson seized his rifle and ran out along the trail with that day's residents of Mariano's fort. The early evening haze was gathering in the valley, but as they gazed down the deeply rutted emigrant road, they could make out an approaching horse and rider.

"Is that ye, Mariano?" the Crow Killer called, his rifle at full-cock.

"Yes, it is I, Señor Liver-Eater," the horseman replied.

As he came closer those who awaited him could see a chief's full regalia lying across the front of Mariano's saddle. He held high a dripping scalp. "This was Captain Jack," he said.

Johnson and Del Gue rode down the valley of the Big Thompson next morning just as the sun rose over the rim of the peaks, the pack horse Mariano had given them loaded down with supplies he had thrown in. Johnson spoke what both of them had thought: "Mariano tol' us he tuk thet skelp four days back, but it wuz fresh."

"Didn't look more'n an hour ol'," Del agreed.

Johnson drew rein, as did his partner then, and dismounted. He pointed at a mass of early fall leaves in their path; as Del bent, he saw that the leaves were spattered with blood.

"Reckon Mariano kilt him hyar?" Del asked.

"Jack ain't dead yit," Johnson said. "Look over yer head, lad." Del crooked his neck.

The gaunt outlines of a giant cottonwood towered there. The cold breeze hissed among the dry leaves remaining on its branches. Far overhead a limb, bent slightly at its outer end, held the swinging body of an Indian, tied hand and foot with rawhide. He had not been hanged by the neck but on plaited rope of rawhide passed beneath his arms and knotted at the back. That he was still alive, the twitchings of his body could attest. That he was still conscious, his direct gaze attested, from black, hate-filled eyes. His lips uttered not a sound. Captain Jack dying in agony was still Captain Jack, the Ute chief.

How any scalped human could have lived all night swinging in the cold wind was more than Del Gue could understand. "I reckon I'll kill ther crittur," he said, throwing rifle to shoulder.

But the Crow Killer savagely struck it down. "Do ye think he'd a-spared Mariano?" He looked up once more at the Ute, then shouted, "How ye feelin', red coon? Is it col' up thar?"

"That war ol' Milt Sublette's trick," Johnson told Del as they rode on. "Ye lasso a high limb, snub yer rope roun' a tree trunk, an' let yer hoss pull it down. Then ye jist tie up yer coon an' tarn it loose."

"Almost as shivery as watchin' ye eat liver," Del told him.

23 The Piegan Princess

CAPTAIN V. T. McGillicuddy, reminiscing in the 1920's, told of Liver-Eating Johnson's part in the great events of the mid-seventies. These were the years in which the Government first closed the Black Hills—the Pa-ha-sa-pa of the Sioux —to settlers, then threw them open once again when the few who had gone in in secret, discovered gold. Those were the years when the Sioux turned from the killing of individual gold hunters to such exploits against the United States Army as those of Crazy Horse and Sitting Bull, and when for one delirious summer and fall victory seemed theirs.

Apparently Johnson scouted in the Hills in 1874. He served as guide for Captain McGillicuddy the next year, in that topographical reconnaissance which so alarmed and enraged the Sioux; McGillicuddy credited him with saving the whole party from annihilation on more than one occasion.[1]

[1] R. W. T. was in constant correspondence with McGillicuddy through the 1920's and has preserved the story of his career as engineer at this period, surgeon-scout for the Second U.S. Cavalry later, and (in Cleveland's first presidency) Agent in charge of the Pine Ridge Reservation, where he established the Sioux Indian Police.

But McGillicuddy apparently never specified just what adventures Johnson went through with his Army engineers, or what might or sagacity he was called upon to exhibit. Nor, tantalizingly enough, is there any story on the record from his assignment in 1876, in charge of the band of Crow scouts who kept surveillance on the Sioux for General Nelson A. Miles. The onetime Crow Killer and his Crow companions in arms— one itches to know details of their working as a team, or even of their talk by the campfires, or even of their sleeping arrangements. But typically enough, the stories of Johnson and the Crows which have survived from the late 1870's concern his individual prowess in hand-to-hand encounter and a special revenge upon the Sioux he undertook for them, quite as if no United States Army existed within a thousand miles. And, typically, the story handed down from the middle 1870's concerns Johnson's traveling not with a whole band of Crow allies but with one Piegan "princess."

White-Eye, whose story this is, was himself in the Hills in 1876, with a party from Fort Laramie which included Wild Bill Hickok, Colorado Charley Utter, Calamity Jane (fresh from the Laramie jail), and some dance-hall girls. But Johnson's adventure for 1876, as described by White-Eye, seems staged against a wilderness still utterly remote from jails and dance halls. And Johnson himself, at fifty-three, is still portrayed as a young man—young enough, indeed, to start Del Gue jumping to conclusions about the Liver-Eater and his twenty-year-old princess.

She looked anything but a princess when Johnson first found her, starved and wizened, on the headwaters of Rosebud creek. Her little brush leanto of broken sticks and twigs was clearly made with her bare hands, for she had been set out on the prairie with no knife. Her skin clothing, in tatters, showed that she had been alone now, exposed to the elements, for weeks. Johnson found her with a crude reed snare, catching what minnows she could in the creek; she would clearly not survive

long on her recent diet. Johnson had little enough respect for
any Piegan—poor relations of the Blackfeet, he thought them.
This wrinkled, haggard woman looked to be seventy.

She knew Johnson, though; he was still exactly the figure
familiar these thirty years in Mountain country. There was not,
according to White-Eye, one gray hair in his red beard or on
his head so miraculously never touched by scalping knife. His
buckskin suit was still filled out, and no more, by his 260 pounds
with no ounce of fat. His weapons—aside from the famous
Bowie he had carried through the Civil War—had changed
ever the years, to be sure; yet the new seemed already legendary.
The Colt Walker with the matching rosewood handle, he had
given to White Badger, the Crow chief who buried Crazy
Woman—and received in return White Badger's stone tomahawk, a tribal antique, its handle richly encased in leather
sewn so delicately that the stitches could hardly be seen and
ornamented as only Crow technique would allow; this ancient
weapon, men knew, Johnson had already wetted with the
blood of Sioux, Cheyenne, and Blackfoot. In more direct replacement of the Colt Walker, he carried a .45 Colt Army,
with swivelled stock lanyard. He still carried the improved
Spencer repeater, replacement for his famous Hawken; the
Army needle gun, he said after testing it extensively, could
"fetch a red nigger es fur as I kin smell one." To his horse, too,
a black stallion hand-picked from the herds of his new friends
the Crows, Johnson attributed some of his own instinct for
sensing the presence of a foe. He sat it in the beautiful saddle
of Anton Sepulveda.

The horse shied and whinnied when Johnson first came upon
the Piegan. Johnson talked with her in sign language, no more
than enough to gather what he had guessed anyway, that it
was Cheyennes who had set her out on the prairie. He gave her
food, then shifted the packs on his lead horse, placing some on
his own mount behind his saddle. She was anxious enough to
ride. She took for granted that she should ride the pack horse

and stay ahead of Johnson, where he could watch her till she proved she could be trusted. Johnson observed soon that she rode well and that despite her recent privations her stamina was extraordinary. Her further qualifications he would observe.

They rode along the Rosebud, where, earlier that summer, Crazy Horse and his warriors had whipped General George Crook. When the trail came to a ford and the Piegan stopped her mount, Johnson waved her on across. That night they camped some thirty-five miles from where the Rosebud enters the Yellowstone. Johnson would let no fire be struck this night, for the country was alive with Indian sign. Since the Custer Massacre had awakened the Indians to a sense of their might, the great mass of Sioux and Cheyenne, numbering many thousands, were dancing under the moon to the greater glory of Crazy Horse, while Sitting Bull, in Canada, was recruiting more followers. Johnson took jerked beef from his saddlebags, along with a little pemmican, and divided the small meal with the Piegan. Then he motioned for her to take his blankets. For himself, in Sioux country and with this unknown woman in his camp, there could be no sleep this night. He sat with his back against a boulder, gun in hand, watching the trail until daylight, catching no more of a catnap than the few moments' dozing he felt safe.

Finally, when darkness and its special dangers had passed, he ordered the squaw to gather twigs. What little smoke rose from these would not be seen far. She made a small fire, and Johnson cooked coffee.

Now the Piegan asked for, and received, Johnson's Bowie knife. Stepping into a thicket, she cut and trimmed a heavy sapling till it formed a serviceable club. She was, after all, but arming herself for a country of constant hazards; Johnson reached into his saddlebags, drew out the famous throwing-knife of Anton Sepulveda, and offered it to her. She took the beautiful blade from its scabbard, then looked at Johnson in some astonishment. Seeing that his purpose was clear, she threw her club aside, fastened Big Anton's scabbard about her waist, slid the weapon back into it, and mounted. The Liver-Eater reminded himself that he must now stay doubly on the alert. Yet, as he studied her tattered back—always enough, he insisted, for him to "tell what an Injun was up ter"—he decided that if she could hold up, the Piegan might make a first-rate traveling companion. He was behind in his mending and tired of cooking.

Johnson was never one to take undue credit. As, thirty-three years before, he had rejected Old Hatcher's credit for strategy against a bear, so in his story of what happened at once that first morning with the Piegan he claimed no credit for saving his own life. The trail turned from the creek bank out over rocks and through thick brush. Simply in order to keep the Piegan in sight, he struck his horse a sharp slap. Then, precisely as the horse leaped ahead, an arrow grazed behind him. The frightened horse plunged, and threw Johnson to the hard-packed earth; he heard the sound of its hoofs pounding away, mingled in with a war whoop. Breath knocked out of his body, he saw through the dust rising round him a young Blackfoot brave. Then a tattered buckskin skirt flashed through the dust. Johnson saw Big Anton's bright long blade once again in a downward stroke. The young Blackfoot coughed and fell grunting across Johnson's still stunned body.

It occurred to Johnson even as, at last, he stirred himself to heave the Blackfoot's body aside, that he no longer need stand watch against his Piegan. Knife in hand, he sprang erect now, but it was the Piegan who, again and again, sank her blade into the Blackfoot's chest. For the first time in his life, Johnson was sure that he could not have saved his own life, that another had saved it for him. He felt some embarrassment but was not sure why—whether that he had needed help or that he had mistrusted the Piegan. He picked up his rifle and turned away to blow dust from the breech. But there was another surprise in store for him.

"Him lone brave," said the Piegan in English, "no more come. Horse in timber."

"I di'n't know ye could talk white, gal," Johnson said now in real astonishment; and one cannot but reflect that a woman who spoke only matters of such import, was to his own heart.

She wiped the bloody blade in a patch of moss, then handed it to Johnson, and pointed at the dead Blackfoot's scalp.

But the Liver-Eater handed it back to her and drew his Bowie. "I dun't like a toothpick fer this job," he said. He took the scalp with one quick slash, then handed it to the Piegan.

They recovered Johnson's horse and the Blackfoot's as well, and the Piegan took the dead warrior's buckskin jacket as well for her own use, along with his knife and his belt. After they were mounted, Johnson handed her the bridle reins of the captured animal and rode ahead, leaving her to trail along, unwatched, behind. He had decided to camp early. He needed sleep, and the Piegan had earned tonight's guard duty.

So, even as the sun dropped below the wide Montana horizon, Johnson and his companion pulled off the trail. Casting caution to the winds, Johnson ordered a fire. After coffee and some jerked meat and a pipe, he took one of the blankets and, he reported later, dropped off to sleep with no effort at all.

He did, though, wake for a moment when the Piegan stamped out the embers of the dying fire. He saw how she took the remaining blanket, propped it against the saddles, and leaned back. He observed appreciatively how, the Army needle gun across her lap, she kept the heavy revolver also ready to hand. Her eyes gleamed against the starlight. She watched the trail unblinking. She was in the same position when the galaxies paled and gave way to the chill Montana dawn.

Johnson and Waving Grass stayed together through one winter's scouting and another's trapping, in the Belt Mountains below old Fort Benton. She did her share of the work, he reported; she made an excellent trapping partner in a time when, with so few animals left, two men could not have worked together with any fair certainty of profit.

Evenings together, even two who spoke so little must come to know one another's stories. Johnson's curiosity did, after all, force him to remark on her knowing English. She had learned while still almost a baby, she said, from a woman her father captured from a burned emigrant train. For Waving Grass was the daughter of a chief; the emigrant woman had remained by rights in his lodge until her death. Waving Grass' own history was no less violent.

She was under ten when the Sioux made one of their periodic raids on her people, camped on the Belle Fourche River, and carried her away. The band which had captured her, under Little Crow, put more than eight hundred settlers and soldiers to horrible deaths in Minnesota that same summer, and the little girl watched, fascinated, the scalp dance which followed. At fourteen she was given to Black Bear, a Sioux warrior. But within the year a Northern Cheyenne, Screeching Cat, took Black Bear's scalp and Black Bear's woman. Among the Cheyennes, Waving Grass would encounter troubles more desperate yet.

For though by Cheyenne tradition Screeching Cat should have taken the girl into his lodge merely as his wife's slave, instead he took her as his second, favored wife. The first wife drove a long, thin blade into the heart of her husband and in punishment was burned at the stake. For her part in the triangle, Waving Grass had been put on the prairie where Johnson found her.

She might, conceivably, have stayed with Johnson for more winters than two, had she not been so markedly young, and a woman. Perhaps Del Gue moved Johnson to sending her off by his mild enough remark that Johnson was furnishing her "with bed and board." Johnson replied "Board but not bed, ol' coon" so decisively that Del dropped the subject; but when, after a fair winter of trapping, they came out of the mountains and sold their fur at a trading post on the Yellowstone, Johnson bade her good-bye.

Or perhaps Waving Grass herself wanted more than a trapping partnership (as indeed she was later to suggest). If so, she had timed her move wrong. The Army had set up a compound at Knife River for the widows and orphans of braves, where they might somehow shift till they could be sorted out. Johnson divided his winter's proceeds equally with his Piegan, packed her bulging supplies on two horses, bought her a new rifle and revolver to protect such wealth, and sent her riding to the compound.

She went to Knife River, proudly, as "Johnson's squaw"—though she can hardly have expected to be welcomed as such by the widows of Blackfeet or Sioux. And the story is told of how Jacob Horner met her there:

A group of soldiers walked over to the Indian camp. Seeing several squaws seated on the ground, one of the cavalrymen remarked to Horner, "How would you like to have a squaw?" To their astonishment, one of the squaws turned and with flashing eyes berated them soundly in good English. She told them, Horner said, that she was the wife of . . . Liver-Eating Johnson.[2]

24 Eight Scalps for the Crows

JOHNSON's destination when he first met the Piegan was a rendezvous on the Musselshell, but at the mouth of the Rosebud he found all who were scheduled to meet at that rendezvous. Yellowstone Kelly, Chief of Scouts to General Nelson

[2] Roy P. Johnson, "Jacob Horner of the 7th Cavalry," in *North Dakota History*, April, 1949.

Miles' command (a position to be held the next year by Johnson) had just come in from the Tongue River, where the Sioux were gathering for what looked like a do-or-die battle. With Kelly were Del Gue and Jim Moorman, another old frontiersman. Some twenty-five Crow scouts were at the camp under the command of their own chief, Black Eagle.

The scouts had gathered a large supply of meat and other provisions. They had more than enough saddle and pack horses. They had a first-rate commander in Kelly. But they also had Sam Grant, terrorizing the Crows. Sam was the especially black Negro who, the year before, had put Charley Siringo, the famous Texas cowboy, "out of active business." If Charley's own story of the event may be prejudiced, it reflects just the reputation which Sam Grant took care to establish for himself.

"I was seated on the ground by the campfire smoking, late in the evening," Siringo wrote in 1885, when Grant "rode up and dismounted. Picking up my pistol, which lay on the opposite side of the fire from where I was sitting, he examined it, then threw it away, at the same time pulling his pistol, with the remark, 'Why don't you have a good one like mine?' He then fired at my heart. My hands were clamped around my left leg—the knee being on a level with my heart. The large dragoon bullet struck the knee, going through and lodging near the skin on the opposite side. He was raising the pistol as though to fire again, Siringo judged, when a cowboy friend of Siringo's—also Negro —galloped up. Grant swore that his pistol had gone off by accident, then galloped away—and sent a doctor out late that night to cut the bullet out of Siringo's knee. Siringo had thirty-five years to ponder Grant's motives before a friend told him (in time for a later version of Siringo's memoirs) that a "certain wealthy cattleman . . . hired Sam Grant" to kill him.[1]

[1] The entire account is in Charles A. Siringo, *A Lone Star Cowboy* (Santa Fe: the author, 1919), pp. 30-31. All but the friend's information as to Grant's motivation appeared also in Siringo's earlier *A Texas Cowboy*.

It was in any event Sam Grant's reputation that he dealt extensively in murder, and that though quarrelsome he preferred to kill in stealth. Town marshals all along the Chisholm Trail had sworn to kill him.

Grant had, it seems, come up the Bozeman Trail with a herd of cattle for the northern Army posts, but had now deserted. Three days before Johnson's arrival he had ridden into the camp of the scouts and attached himself to them. Though advised by Kelly that his services were not needed, he had simply grinned, announced himself as staying regardless, and added that he knew how to kill Indians. Somehow he persuaded the Crows that he was as interested in killing them as in killing Sioux. By the time Johnson came into camp, Jim Moorman could tell him that the Crows wanted "ter tie up an' burn the varmint."

Johnson was seated on the ground among the Crow scouts, smoking with Black Eagle against his buffalo-skin tepee, while Moorman spoke. He had been watching with satisfaction how capably Waving Grass could broil antelope steak. Now he looked at Black Eagle and the other Crow warriors scattered about. But either they had not heard Moorman, or they had nothing to add. Action about Sam Grant would be up to Johnson.

"Burnin's too cruel," Johnson said. He saw Moorman's astonishment. "Whar is this black galoot?"

"Amongst them trees," Moorman said, "camped alongside ther spring. Sez he mought git mad an' pizen ther water."

"He'll never pizen yer water," Johnson promised, "les'n by his carcass floatin' in it. Ye know, I ain't et sin' yesterday." He ate the steaks Waving Grass brought him, slowly, with relish. The Crows sat round him, waiting with anticipation his equally slow approach to Sam Grant.

Now the legend has it that Johnson was curious, having never seen a Negro before; and indeed he likely had seen none since coming West. The cowboy that he saw now was seated in a clearing among the pines, mending his saddlebags and quite unconscious of Johnson's approach. A short distance away, beyond the trees, his horse nosed aside dry leaves to get at the sparse grass. Grant was a big man physically, rusty black in color. He was dressed in cowboy jeans and flannel shirt; his wide belt held two pistols and a large Bowie. He hummed as he plied his needle, and his white teeth flashed. Suddenly he looked up, and Johnson saw how his eyes expressed amazement. He had heard no sound, yet this stranger stood beside him. Grant dropped his sewing and looked around him. Indian faces, Crow faces in war paint, peered from among the trees. "Them won't hurt ye," the white stranger said as Sam Grant rose to his feet. "Them is hyar ter see me move ye on down ther road."

Sam Grant looked into the stranger's strange, hard eyes and looked away. But he said, "Reckon yer don't know who I am, white man."

There was a guffaw from among the trees. Del Gue and Jim Moorman came forward now. (Yellowstone Kelly, to their regret, was out of camp since morning and so could not see the fun.)

"Reckon it's t'other way roun', black feller," Jim said. "Reckon *ye* don't know Johnson hyar."

Grant put his hand on a pistol butt.

Johnson stood with thumbs hooked in his belt. "Ther hell with who ye air," he said. "I'm offerin' ye yer life. Now git on yer hoss an' git outen hyar."

Sam Grant drew his right-hand pistol, fast, but in too close quarters. As the gun left its holster Johnson seized Grant's wrist, stepping to one side as Grant's bullet dug into the ground. Still holding Grant's wrist in an iron grip with his own right hand, Johnson grasped his opponent's neck now with his left, and with that leverage threw both their weights upon the Negro's gun arm. Grant's elbow cracked and snapped. Despite what must have been terrible pain, he reached for his left-hand gun. But swiftly the Liver-Eater backheeled him, threw him some ten feet, and drew his stone tomahawk. Hurled from a distance of about ten feet, the terrible weapon turned over once and struck the Negro fairly between the eyes.

Jim Moorman withdrew the tomahawk from Sam Grant's skull as the Crows crowded around. Waving Grass took the weapon from Jim's hand and carried it to the spring to wash off the blood. Johnson turned to Black Eagle. "Ye kin hev his skelp, an' his hoss an' weppins," he said.

Johnson's finding the Crows where he did had been pretty much accidental, and in a few days all but Black Eagle and some half-dozen of his braves had gone on to their encampment on Big Dry Creek, just off the Missouri, where they could keep in daily contact with the Army of the Frontier. The seven Crows who remained, along with Johnson, Moorman, and Del Gue, were to rejoin their fellows as soon as they had accumulated a large enough supply of fresh meat in daily hunting trips from their camp.

One moonless night Del, on guard duty while the rest skinned out the meat, heard a moan of pain from the darkness. Del at once dropped to the ground and worked himself noiselessly toward the sound. As he approached a dry gully leading up from the river, he saw a form crawling toward him. Circling, he came up behind the moving creature. It was a white woman he found, delirious, scalped alive; taking the chance that her Indian foe was closer than his own friends, he nevertheless raised the alarm.

Johnson was the first to appear. He shouted orders to the Crow scouts to chase down the Sioux who had scalped the woman. Waving Grass, preparing a dressing for the woman's head, somehow brought her to lucidity. Johnson saw that she must die in a few minutes and set to learning her story. She was, he learned, the one survivor of three families from the Great Bend of the Musselshell. Five days ago seven Sioux had struck and killed, then started with her for their camp on the Tongue River. Then, changing their minds about her, they had scalped her. Somehow she had broken away and crawled, she was sure, at least two miles.

"Seven Sioux—an' two miles," Johnson said to Del Gue. They carried the woman into camp, told Waving Grass to minister to her wants, then saddled horses and rode northward up the Porcupine. Though midnight had passed, the sky was clear and they could see their way. The Crows came back in to report that no Sioux remained in the area. But Johnson sent them out again. "If'n we kin fin' out whar she war skelped, we've got it," he said, "we kin tell whar they's headed."

Del and Jim Moorman thought there was no secret as to the Indians' destination. "They wuz a-headin' fer ther Tongue, di'n't she say?"

"Now, Jim, now, Del," Johnson said. "This coon thort ye knew red niggers better nor thet. We'll wait hyar an' see what ther Crows fin' out."

Black Eagle and his few warriors were gone little more than an hour before they rode back in silently, suddenly, out of the gloom. One of the Crows, The Owl, handed two objects to Johnson; in the dim light the Liver-Eater could barely make them out: the charred stick from a campfire, and a leaf heavy with thickened blood.

"Whar away?" Johnson asked.

The Owl pointed westward.

"Ye see," Johnson told his friends. "Them Sioux is back-trackin'. They know we got the woman's story."

"So they's a-tryin' ter ambush us whar they killed her folks?" Del said.

"Su'thin' like thet," Johnson said. "Lead on, Owl!"

"They named thet Injun right," said Moorman.

They rode slowly through the rest of that night, with The Owl halting now and then to search out the sign. After the sky lightened, they rode at a sharp trot, with The Owl hardly glancing at the ground. Stopping only for meals and for one short rest, they rode all that day and through the next night.

Once they saw a large band of Sioux, more than five hundred warriors with their entire village trailing along behind, hauling their belongings on travois. "They's headed ter join Crazy Horse at Wolf Mountain," Johnson said.

"Hedn't we better tell Kelly?" Del suggested.

But Johnson had more faith in the chief of scouts. "Yallerstun will sight 'em hisself an' report," he said. The seven Sioux whom they were trailing back to the Great Bend of the Musselshell had made no effort to join in with this Sioux village on the move, nor would Johnson now turn aside.

In their second cold gray dawn, The Owl returned from scouting ahead to report that he had reached the cabins. "White squaw know how to count," he said. "Five braves sleep in one cabin. Two watch." The other cabins in the settlement had been burned to the ground.

Johnson suggested now that they cut at once to the riverbank and come up on the Sioux through a narrow belt of timber; his companions agreed.

"Dah-pih-ehk," Black Eagle said, "save one. No kill all."

They left their horses about a half-mile down the river from the cabins and crept up through willows until they were within two hundred yards. They could see three dead bodies piled together behind the single cabin that still stood. Two sentries still paced as The Owl had described them, but soon one squatted to work the breech of his rifle.

Johnson, head propped on his left elbow, surveyed the scene. He silently worked the block on his .56 caliber buffalo gun, then twisted around to face his companions. "I'll tek ther walkin' coon," he said, "an' Del kin git t'other. Try an' git them other coons in ther legs."

The white scouts and the Crow warriors settled themselves on their stomachs, looking over the barrels of their rifles.

"Now, Del," Johnson said. The roar of needle gun and Winchester followed his words at once.

The Indian working on his rifle sat for a few seconds' time without uttering a sound, then toppled over. The heavy bullet from Johnson's rifle plowed through the head of the other sentry; though his skull was smashed, some reflex caused him to stand straight as if alive before toppling into the sandy earth.

One by one the five warriors in their cabin broke into the open, only to receive the combined fire of the party in the timber. Breaking cover at last, the Crows raced across the sand toward where their enemies lay. Two of the five had been killed outright; a third died before the Crows could reach him. Of the remaining two, Johnson was first to reach one, wounded in both legs and in the shoulder; Johnson tomahawked him even as he sang the first note of his death song. The last of the seven Sioux warriors, though both his legs were broken, tried to raise his rifle. But Black Eagle knocked the weapon from his grasp and quickly scalped him. The victim was disabled and maimed, but he could still witness what special ceremony Black Eagle had planned for him.

"Dah-pih-ehk," Black Eagle cried, "will you help to avenge your brothers the Crows?"

Johnson knew Black Eagle's intent, knew what sort of Crow vengeance could be accomplished only by the Crow Killer. For through the years of his and their feuding, the Crows had suffered the contempt of many tribes but above all that of the Sioux. He drew his Bowie.

Leaning now over one of the dead warriors, slowly, expertly, so that all might see his proficiency, he made the necessary incision. Reaching in, he drew out a Sioux liver. The Crow warriors stood proudly erect, watching the proceedings and watching, in the same moment, how the one surviving Sioux watched too. The onetime Crow Killer stood now in front of this scalped and suffering Sioux brave. Holding the liver on high, he brought it down to his mouth; he bit. Then, grimacing, he spat. He threw the organ into the face of the watching Sioux brave.

"Thet thar ain't fitten fer a dog ter eat," said Johnson.

The Crows took their live captive down the river, where Johnson and Moorman and Gue could not see their final treatment of him. The trappers dug one common grave for the white settlers whose bodies they gathered. Finally they dragged the bodies of the six dead Sioux into the cabin four of them had slept in, and burned the cabin down.

The three Mountain Men rode ahead of the Crows as the party started back for their camp on the Big Porcupine. Seven Sioux scalps flapped from the headstalls of seven Crow bridles. Black Eagle rode ahead to say to the Liver-Eater, "Dah-pih-ehk, for this the Absaroka thank you."

Del Gue is witness that Johnson looked away for a moment before he answered Black Eagle, toward the south, toward the valley of the Little Snake, perhaps, where young Crow warriors had incurred his enmity thirty years before. But Johnson's eyes were unfathomable.

"Ther Crows don't owe me nothin'," he replied.

part five

The Old Trapper

25 Burial for Bear Claw

AFTER THE winter campaign of 1876–77, the power of the Indians of the Northwest began a steady decline; the victory of General Miles at Wolf Mountain broke the spirit of Crazy Horse and many of his allies. With the passing of Sioux might, too, began the passing of the life Johnson and his friends had known. Though the rounding up of hostile tribes was to take many months, and though indeed there were occasional uprisings and massacres for some fifteen years, settlers and gold hunters and even cattlemen with great herds from Texas swarmed into what had been a wilderness. No doubt the new arrivals found the plains and mountains primeval in their vastness, but for oldtime trappers the oldtime feeling of their country had gone. This was the last of the frontier, and they were the last of the frontiersmen. Few of them could be termed "old men," yet they had lived beyond their time. The newcomers, and especially the cowboys, they thought of as "pilgrim tenderfoots."

In the fall of 1878, Del Gue and Hatchet Jack found Liver-Eating Johnson camped at Pryor's Fork on the Yellowstone. The three talked over prospects. Fur was scarce, and scalps scarcer. Even proper equipment was hard to come by: Jack, replacing a worn-out hatchet, could find only a model better suited to the driving of nails than "fer choppin' Injuns." But with three large pack horses in tow, the partners set out for the Little Rockies, below Milk River, near Bear Claw's canyon. Crossing the Yellowstone, then four forks of the Musselshell, and finally the Missouri at Johnson's old woodyard, they reached their destination without incident. Some time before spring, they promised themselves, they would go learn whether Bear Claw was in his winter retreat once more. But first, they must get their own winter's work under way.

Del Gue picked out their camp site, for he had come here before with that master trapper Old Mizzou. Del led his partners to a clear, cold spring in the rocks on the southern slope of the range. While they were building their cabin there, still in mid-October, a light snow fell; they agreed that despite the general scarcity of furs so early a snow was an omen of good trapping. Indeed Johnson and Jack brought in a large catch the very first week. Del, taking his turn as hunter and cook and skinner for the outfit, had plenty to do.

All went well, with no sign of Indians to worry or interest the trappers, until mid-December. Then one evening Del reported that, returning from his day's hunt with the shoulder of an elk, he had heard the discharge of a gun at a distance. Likely Bear Claw, Del suggested, though the incident must be looked into.

"Ye kin tek ther trap lines t'morrer, Del," Johnson said. "Thet warn't Chris a-shootin'. He long ago laid up his meat fer ther winter. We'll tek ther trail in ther mornin', Jack."

Next morning, while the stars still shone, Johnson and Hatchet Jack followed Del's well-beaten trail back into the hills till they found where, the day before, he had broken across the packed snow. They went on in his steps till they found the remains of the elk which he had cached in a tree. More than one shoulder had been cut; both shoulders, both hams were gone.

"Three red coons on foot, Jack," Johnson read the signs. He knelt to study further. "Blackfoots," he announced. "They heerd Del shoot but got hyar arter he left. Del was sure in luck."

Hatchet Jack quivered like a hound on the leash. "Come on, Liver-Eatin'," he said. "They mought hev foun' ol' Chris."

Rifles in hand, they followed the trail at a trot, the hard-caked snow hissing and crackling under their moccasined feet. The Blackfeet's trail led them at last to a broad and shallow canyon. As they rounded one of the many turns they saw, set into a natural niche in the rock wall, a tidy little cabin. But the door stood open. They ran forward to the threshold.

Nothing inside—not the pole bunk, not the roughly fashioned chair or the small table, not the bear-claw necklaces on the cabin walls—seemed to have been disturbed except its owner. Old Bear Claw Chris lay on the earthen floor, his head all clotted blood. One hand held a partly completed necklace of bear claws; other claws, shaken loose from the buckskin thong upon which the old man had been threading them, were scattered over the floor. Chris had not known he was an Indian's target, but had kept at his work till his moment came.

Johnson probed in the front wall until he found a crack where the chinks had fallen from between the logs; Chris' failure to watch for the cracks had of course been his death. The heavy-caliber bullet had come from the outside and had not stopped in Chris' skull. Johnson sighted roughly, then walked to where the bullet had stopped in the far wall and dug it out with his Bowie.

"Needle gun," he said.

Hatchet Jack cursed.

"Some day, Jack, I air a-goin' ter quit huntin' red niggers, an' kill off them renegade traders," Johnson promised.

"Thar's two sells rifles to Injuns down by Fort Peck," Jack said. "I'll pole thar heads."

The body of old Chris was still warm. He had died only this morning, and now Johnson and Jack could piece together that whole night's history. For the Blackfeet's trail to the cabin led in only the one direction; they had come upon Chris' cabin only after yesterday's hunting. They had come into the same country where Del hunted from another direction. They had run to where they heard Del's shot, then lain in wait until darkness, hoping to ambush the hunter. When that hope failed them, they cut off the remaining shoulder and the two hams and started back for their camp, across country. Their discovery of Bear Claw had been sheer accident. They stayed all night by the cabin, hoping that its owner would open the door. Knowing that other trappers were nearby, they were too smart to fire the cabin. But come early morning, light from inside the cabin shone through the crack in the log wall. One of the Indians shot Chris. Then all three smashed his door open, and he who had shot Chris scalped him.

Johnson looked around the cabin walls, to study what loot the Blackfeet might have taken.

"Them wuz Bear Claw's pretties," Jack said of the necklaces hanging there.

Johnson shook his head. "These hyar lack matchin' claws," he said. "Ye'll see thet the Blackfoots got his best." He lifted Chris' head once more and pointed at the bloody clot where the scalp had been taken. "Looks like ol' Mose looked," Johnson said, and Hatchet Jack nodded.

Only now did the morning sun top the peaks, but even so early they were hours too late. They hurried from the cabin and along the Blackfeet's clear trail. The Indians had horses now: Chris', no doubt. Suddenly Johnson stopped dead in his tracks, and Jack behind him. Johnson sniffed the air. "This child smells smoke," he said. They walked on more cautiously now to the rim of a canyon. There they looked down on their Blackfeet.

Having breakfasted, the three warriors were wrestling with a great trunk-like box. While one held the bridle of Chris' skittish pack horse, the other two tried to tie on the load.

The two trappers lay on their bellies and sighted down the heavy rifle barrels. "In ther shoulder," Jack urged, and Johnson nodded; they would put these Blackfeet out of action without killing them outright. And as their blasting shots echoed around the walls of the canyon, one of the packers and the warrior who held the bridle spun and fell heavily, their entire right shoulders blown away. The frantic pack horse tore loose; the heavy box fell on the one uninjured Blackfoot. Johnson slid a long, heavy cartridge into his rifle, dropped the breechblock, took a quick aim, and fired. All three Indians were disabled now. The trappers climbed leisurely down from the rocks to the canyon floor.

With one swift blow of his hatchet Jack broke the big box open. Chris Lapp's lifework lay before their eyes.

"Finished pieces," Johnson said. "All matched claws." As he'd told Jack, the Blackfeet had Chris' best.

Jack put up his hatchet and drew his knife. Soon enough, the three Blackfeet must bleed to death from their shoulder wounds. All three sang their death songs. Jack stepped up to one of them, ran his blade into the eye socket, and flipped the eyeball upon the ground. His victim flinched but made no more sound than a grunt.

"Fergot somethin'," Jack announced. Replacing the knife and drawing his hatchet, he scalped the Blackfeet, lifting each from the ground by his topknot and whacking the scalps off close to their skulls with the heavy blade. "Thet's fer Mad Mose," he said. Now he took their eyes too. But finally, at Johnson's urging, he went his rounds once more to chop off and collect their heads. It was a shame, Jack said, not to let them wait for their death. Johnson told him only that they must waste no more time, for they still had hours of work to be done that day.

Johnson lifted Chris' trunk and, with Jack holding the bridle, threw it on the skittish pack-horse's back and tied it on securely. Then each caught a saddled horse, mounted, and with the pack horse in tow rode out of that canyon and back to Bear Claw's. Jack threw his three heads on the ground beside the cabin. Both trappers then carried Chris outside, and brought huge armfuls of brush and dry saplings. Firing the cabin, they threw yet more of the brush into the open doorway. Now they must sit by the smoking ashes for hours to allow the frozen earth to thaw.

At last they raked ashes and embers to one side and dug Chris' grave. Jack went down the canyon to a stand of box elders, and cut some stakes. They wrapped Bear Claw in his own blankets, leaving only his face exposed, and set him into the earth.

"Thutty-five y'ars I knowed this coon," Johnson said. "Fust met 'im on ther Green River. He says ter me . . . ," and Jack joined in with Johnson, "Great Jehosophat, Pocahontas, an' John Smith."

Jack removed an armful of necklaces from Chris' box and strewed them into the grave. Next he lifted the box and turned the rest of its contents out upon the ground.

"Wa'al now," said Johnson. He stooped and picked up a scalp. Jack spread out other scalps, more than a hundred, braided and oiled and hooped.

"Never sol' a skelp in his life," Jack said. "Kep' 'em all shined up wi' his pretties."

They tossed these trophies too into the grave and, over all, the loose dirt from Bear Claw's floor. When they had raised a cairn of stones, Jack dug three holes, one each at side and head and foot. Here he planted his sharpened box-elder stakes. On these he jammed down his three Blackfeet heads. At last he stepped back to admire his work. "Ye know, Liver-Eater," he said, "Injun heads looks better wi'out any eyes."

Del, trying to run two men's trap lines that day, had as much work as he could handle. He had the feeling that his partners had run into trouble, and hurried so that he might be ready to help when they came in. Even so, he did not get back to the cabin until long after dark; when he did return, he found that his friends, for all their adventures, had had the shorter day. The whale-oil lamp was already lighted. Hot juicy steaks waited for Del on the fire, and biscuits as only the Liver-Eater could brown them.

A blizzard raged that night, shaking the new-made cabin to its stone foundations, but the big fireplace glowed. Along with their tales of Bear Claw, they had winters' cold to remember. Johnson said he remembered a much colder Christmas season: that when Portuguese Phillips rode to Laramie Fort. Del said that as far as he was concerned the coldest winter ever was that through which Johnson trekked from Blackfoot captivity.

In their reminiscing, they none of them knew that another of their mountain comrades had died late that summer. Against all

Mountain Man tradition, Mariano Modeno had taken off his moccasins and lain down on his own front porch to die.

True to his word, Hatchet Jack performed one more vengeance for Bear Claw and for all the Mountain Men whom Indians had shot with rifles. He sought out the traders who had sold needle guns to three Blackfeet, killed them, and poled their heads above Fort Peck.

26 Sheriff Johnson

WITH Bear Claw dead, and Mariano, Liver-Eating Johnson and Del Gue were "old" trappers, though to be sure Johnson is described as having all the vigor of a man in his prime, even in his middle sixties. After their excellent winter's catch, Johnson moved away from old haunts. He stopped in long enough at Leadville, Colorado, for White-Eye Anderson to report on his doings. His official duties in Coulson, Montana, appear in that town's newspapers. Finally he was to seek "stompin' room" far northwest, in Alberta.

Leadville, far up in the Colorado mountains, won its fame almost overnight as a place where fortunes could be made and lost in a moment's play. Here came Welsh miners and other European immigrants willing to spend their waking hours underground, at the sort of labor native-born Americans shunned. Here came gamblers and confidence men from the Eastern seaboard. Desperadoes and hired killers roamed the streets day and night, and prostitutes arrived by every stage. Highwaymen sold their loot, and ambushers sold their services, in the center of town. From such older diggings as Alder Gulch and Deadwood came all manner of swindlers, for in Leadville they could win their fast buck faster yet. Buckskin leggings and moccasins were reflected now in patent leather shoes.

There were honest investors in Leadville, to be sure (and these must be on the lookout for a knife thrust in the dark). And there were Mountain Men who had come just to see the diggings, quiet bearded men in buckskin, disturbed because disturbance had come to their mountains but competent to look out for themselves. They were, no doubt, mere figures from a vanished past; but the new breed of outlaws and killers walked carefully around them and avoided exchange with their scalping knives and tomahawks and Hawkens and Springfields.

White-Eye Jack and his partner Yankee Judd were in Leadville as foremen in the great Bull's Eye mine. Judd had protested the move to Leadville, even after White-Eye portrayed the usual end of a trapper—scalpless, rotting in some lonely gulch, a feast for the buzzards. Finally Judd had agreed that he would work the mines, but only in the summer; come winter, he would be off trapping once more. The partners worked the same shift and roomed together over the saloon of Rowdy Joe Gow, a gunman from Newton, Kansas, recommended to them by his friendship for their friend, the late Wild Bill Hickok. Across the street from them, this August, lived twenty Cheyenne warriors, in town nominally for provisions but actually for arms and ammunition. Hanging Kettle, their chief, was all opulent respectability in his tall beaver hat, with four eagle feathers protruding.

One morning in late August, just off their shift at the mine and cleaning up in their room, White-Eye and Judd heard unusual bedlam in the streets. Peering out their only window, they could see only that the Cheyennes had deserted their camp. Buckling on their gun belts, they raced to the street.

Pushing their way through the hard-packed crowd, White-Eye and Judd found Liver-Eating Johnson and, at his feet, two burly but now motionless miners. White-Eye knew them as fighters and troublemakers from his own shift, Lavery and Morgan.

Johnson stood silhouetted against the buffalo-hide tepees of the Cheyennes, gazing steadily at Bill Greiner, the sheriff of Eagle County. Back against the crowd stood Del Gue, leaning on his own rifle and Johnson's with a half-grin on his leathern face.

Greiner was a powerful man known for his mettle. Give or take ten pounds, he was as big as Johnson. It was said of him that he rarely had to use his Colt's pistol; it was said that he could subdue a half-dozen ordinary men with his bare hands.[1] His sheriff's star shone splendidly in the morning sun, and he looked Johnson full in the face.

"We can't have our citizens knocked around like this, stranger," Bill Greiner said quietly.

"Then ye'd better keep 'em off'n me," Johnson said. "I ain't kilt nobody hyar—not yit. But them tenderfoots shoved ag'in me. I jist knocked their heads tergither."

A dozen Mountain Men in the audience roared approval, and the Sheriff thought to tell them that these were not tenderfeet but miners.

"All town pilgrims air tenderfoots," Johnson said. "If'n any but tenderfoots shoved ag'in me like thet, they'd be dead coons now."

Del Gue chuckled. White-Eye, beside him, wondered if perhaps he might head off trouble by telling the Sheriff who Johnson was. But now an aged and dignified Cheyenne came through the crowd. Yankee Judd whispered to Del, "Thet's Hangin' Kittle, the chief."

Johnson half turned to greet the old man. "How air ye, Hangin' Kittle?" he asked.

The old chief craned his neck to see who had recognized him. "Dah-pih-ehk Absaroka," he exclaimed. Then he said to Bill Greiner, "This is the killer of Crows. He is the Great White Chief of the Shoshoni. His victims are strewn in all the moun-

---

[1] Statement of Mrs. J. Da Lee, Greiner's sister-in-law, of Red Cliff, Colorado.

tains and the plains. My grandsons, great warriors, were not born when he took the trail of the Crows, and my sons were still but boys."

"What has this to do with me?" Greiner said.

The old chief stood tall to express his scorn. "Dah-pih-ehk will kill you with one hand," he said. "White law man, you are only a papoose."

For once, Bill Greiner's eyes blazed at a challenge. He turned from the chief who had so disparaged his might, back to the Mountain Man who knocked "town pilgrims" about. "So you are Liver-Eating Johnson," he said.

Johnson agreed that he was. Then, looking Greiner over with some honest admiration, he said, "Ye air 'bout ther biggest papoose this child ever seed. Air we a-goin' ter hug?"

For a moment the sheriff did want fight. Then anger left his face and he put out his hand. "I don't think we'll hug," he said. "Welcome to Leadville, Johnson." The two miners, regaining consciousness, were trying to get on their feet. Johnson wrapped his powerful fingers around the neck of each, raised them, set them down on their feet with a jar the bystanders felt, and sent them running. Then he and the sheriff warmly shook hands

Johnson rather enjoyed the three weeks he and Del spent in Leadville. They looked in on such former Mountain Men as White-Eye, Texas Jack Omohundro, and Colorado Charley Utter, who had quit their trapping and become "tenderfoots." Johnson, as Bill Greiner's guest, watched with admiration how the sheriff handled his rough element. Even Del, watching stagecoach arrivals, was entertained to see eyeglasses and canes and tan shoes, and the waistcoated big bellies of investors and the painted cheeks of dance-hall girls. But the investors looked through Del as if he were not there. Worse, the girls looked at Del more intently than he liked. "If'n I wanted weemen, I'd grab me one," he said, "but I'm danged if'n any air a-goin' ter grab me." Del urged Johnson to get back into such wilderness as still existed in the West, and Johnson was willing.

The partners rode north into Wyoming. Del was made no happier to see a herd of long-horned cattle on the Bozeman Trail above Fort Laramie. If he had his way, he said, he'd feed "ther hull bunch" strychnine. Johnson fell in with Del's mood. "They'll be a-wantin' us ter milk 'em next," he said. "Warn't nobody on this Bozeman Trail when ther Sioux wuz out," he said. "Nobody but me an' Portygee Phillips."

The Northern Pacific Railroad, too, stretched toward the Yellowstone, drew their rancor. They agreed that life would not be worth living when one did not have to defend it.

At the Powder River the partners turned right to follow its course. After several more days in the saddle they arrived at Fort Keogh. There a frontiersman gave Johnson a message that Del took as another sign of the West's miserable change: Sheriff Tom Irvine of Custer County had appointed Johnson his deputy at Coulson. Del wanted no part of that railroad town's desperadoes, though Johnson said that what Greiner could do at Leadville with two hands he could do at Coulson with only one, and so "rest up" for further adventures.

"But s'pose ye air called on ter kill a white man?" Del asked, in obvious appeal to Johnson's boast that he never had.[2]

"I reckon ez how I kin keep them galoots in line wi'out killin' 'em," was Johnson's only answer.

[2] After all, Johnson had other ways of handling troublemakers. Doc Carver heard Johnson's rationale spelled out clearly at the time of their first meeting. According to the Carver mss., p. 36, he and Johnson were introduced by Dave Perry. ("Dave was called the 'bad man' of North Platte because he had shot a few men, but I know personally that they needed killing.")

"Dave introduced me to a big man with a heavy red beard and said he was Liver-Eating Johnson. . . . There was a hide-hunter down there said that he had shook down Whistler's squaw's corpse from a tree where she was resting on the Republican; Mexican dollars, about 200, had been buried with [her] to make her journey easier. . . . Some of the men wanted to hang the hide-hunter right then and there, but Johnson said it was too much trouble over nothing and threw the fellow out. The door was shut and when the hide-man hit it, it came off the hinges."

Johnson's decision was firm: He accepted his appointment as deputy. But so was Del's decision firm: He set off for the Platte.

Johnson was a popular deputy with just one element in Custer County, the ordinary citizen who wanted peace. The hardened desperadoes left town when he moved in—and the Sheriff objected that Johnson made too few arrests, and so took in too few fees. Irvine came all the way from Miles City to investigate. Overtaking Johnson on his rounds, he asked him about the roughing up of various prisoners which had come to his ears, and their later release.

Johnson explained lightly: "Shucks, Tom, them wuzn't bad 'uns, jist likkered up. I allus teks ther two wust 'uns an' bumps ther heads tergether. That settles it. I kin keep peace among these hyar pilgrims." [3]

Irvine told Johnson that all lawbreakers must be arrested and sent to Miles City, but Johnson held to his own ways: He "didn't wanter mek ther county stand a feed bill on ornery pilgrims." The sheriff recognized defeat, recognized that as long as he had Johnson as deputy he would have Johnson's manner of law enforcement, and took the next stage back home.

At that, Irvine was in Coulson long enough to see that Johnson was effective. "These hyar pilgrims" crossed the street to stay away from him, but Eastern "tenderfoots" followed him all around town. ("Ever time I tarns aroun' I steps on a tenderfoot's tender foot," was Johnson's homemade jest.) They gawked at this giant's buckskins weekdays and seemed to find just as much to gawk at on Sundays, when his red beard was set off by an old blue broadcloth coat, with pants to match. Johnson still wore his double moccasins, and even with his tenderfeet tagging along behind he could somehow appear without warning in the midst of deadly argument. "Wa'al boys," he'd tell the principals as he thrust them apart, "this hez gone far 'nuff. An' whichever

[3] *Carbon County Democrat,* Red Lodge, Montana, February 7, 1900.

coon don't like thet, kin meet me now, hyar on ther spot, wi' fists, knives, clubs, or guns."

Soon men bent on fighting planned their fight quietly, then conducted it out of town. "Ef'n one galoot wants ter kill another galoot, thet's his right," Johnson said. "But Tom said ter keep these squabbles off'n ther streets."

Conceivably Johnson would have had to kill on the job after all, if he had been in town the day Henry Lumpp, drunk, shot and killed Johnson's deputy-helper, "Muggins" Taylor. A bartender arrested Lumpp and sent him off to Irvine in Miles City before Johnson could return.

Johnson did a good job, then, by his own lights, and a good enough job by Tom Irvine's so that he was left in office. But Johnson longed for his wilderness. Old cronies visited him, to urge him back among them. And old Wind River Jake came in with a specific invitation.

Johnson said later that he had been in a black mood, "wond'rin what I war a-comin' ter" in a town, when he saw Jake riding up the narrow street. "I kim outer it then," he said, "fer I seen right hyar a tarnin' point." More literally, he saw how Jake's old back was no longer erect in the saddle. He saw that Jake's hair, "whut nary Injun ever fetched," had gone long and scraggly in the twenty years since they had seen one another, and how the wrinkles had covered his face.

Jake reined in where Johnson was standing, and despite his age he sprang nimbly from his horse. "I'm clean up frum ther Platte, Liver-Eatin'," he cried. "I hev brought ye news from Del."

Johnson embraced the old man in his bear's grip. "Hyar ye air, Jake, lookin' younger'n ye war when we poled Ther Wolf. Ye 'member?" And indeed they could have reminisced, but it was plans for the winter ahead that Jake had come in to discuss.

Arkansas Pete was on Milk River, across into Canada, Jake said, getting set for a winter's trapping. Now Jake came to the point: Pete was building not for himself alone but for two, "An' Pete says fer ye ter git on outen hyar. Says ye air a Mounting Man, not a tenderfoot. He says yer ter meet him on Milk River."

Jake had begun the delivery of his message in the shade of the feed store where he first met Johnson. He pursued its importance in Johnson's shack of an office, behind the store. Scanning the faces of wanted men on Johnson's posters, he brought out another argument: "Them's all took keer uv."

"Is Del a-goin' along, Jake?" Johnson wanted to know.

Not unless Johnson would, Jake said, "An' he said ye wouldn't. I'm a-goin' back ter ther Platte."

They puffed on their pipes for a spell. "All took keer uv," Jake said once again. "They don't need no orficer hyar."

They went out into the stable. Johnson's powerful coal-black horse whinnied and rubbed its nose on Johnson's shoulder. "Whar'd ye git ther hoss?" asked Jake. Johnson said that a rancher had given him the horse because he admired it so. "Is thet all?" Jake asked, doubtfully, and drew Johnson's admission that he had helped the rancher out "a leetle when he war a-playin' poker wi' a card sharp."

The next day Jake started back for the Platte, shrewdly confident that when Del reached Arkansas Pete's place, in Milk River country, he would find Johnson already there. Johnson did send in his resignation. He re-covered Big Anton's saddle for a few more years' use. He laid in a good supply of rifle and revolver ammunition. He took down and honed the blade of his Bowie. On a fine, crisp fall morning just one year after he reached Coulson, he mounted his big black, took the reins of his pack horse in hand, and set off into the wild free wind which blew from the mountains northwest. He had entered his last phase.

27 Last Trail

"WA'AL, GUESS he's gone up to Milk River, shore," said the early-day trapper when asked about a companion's absence. Now the Upper Milk became the last stamping ground of the Rocky Mountain Man, stretching across the vast, almost treeless plains of Alberta. The country had been trapped by Hudson's Bay men for more than a century, but the Company had worked millions of square miles more.

Arkansas Pete had set out with plenty of time that summer. He built him a house that was snug and secure, and bigger than any he had ever seen. There was one big room with four long bunks in it, two on either side of the big fireplace and chimney. Smaller rooms were to hold gear and furs. The stake fence and the swinging gate on its hide hinges were not devised to keep out enemies (for that would have been impossible) but to keep Pete's stock in where Pete could see them. Inland from the river, still Pete had built on a low bluff where he could see for miles along the Milk. Now Pete need only locate his trap lines before the snows could hide the land's distinguishing characteristics, thinking the while of the stories he and Liver-Eating Johnson would have to tell one another through the long winter's nights. Pete knew that Johnson could not possibly resist the attractions of Milk River, after a year's horrible gentility as a town galoot.

Despite his seventy years, Pete was wiry and full of vigor. His hair was gray and hung down to his waist. His mustache and beard were grayer still from wind and weather, and tidily trimmed with his pair of shears. He carried with him a Mormon Bible which his old comrade Mormon Jack gave him, having stolen two from a Church. Neither could read, but Pete and Jack had a more learned friend teach them whole passages and then mark their Bibles to show them which passage was which. Pete would saddle his horse, mount, and ride to the top of the bluff just above a copse of willows and cattails. Then he looked up and down the river but saw nothing that he had not seen the day before. On his last morning alive he sniffed the air and decided snow was in the offing. That morning would be bright, he saw, as soon as the mist left the water. He opened his Bible and began to "read." Perhaps Pete was old enough, or sure enough of his own luck after so many years, or confident enough while reading his Bible, to neglect a careful watch. While he recited from the Psalms, his old gray head bent, a rifle barrel emerged from the copse below him. The rifle spoke, and as its report echoed, Pete raised both hands over his head, still clutching his Bible, and pitched from his horse. The horse whinnied in fear and trotted off.

The young Assiniboine warrior who sprang from his copse now found that his heavy bullet had torn clear through Pete's ribs and heart and lungs. He took Pete's scalp and weapons and decided against the Bible. He caught Pete's mount, brought his own well-trained horse from where it had been lying, and led both into Pete's stockade. He must have been watching Pete long enough to be sure he had no partner in the hills, for he worked methodically among Pete's belongings, loading them on two of Pete's extra horses. He finished Pete's biscuits. Last he tied Pete's stiffening scalp to his bridle and, riding his own animal, led Pete's four horses away into the north.

As the sun rose high that day, the Indian and his *remuda* vanished over the horizon. After night fell and the loons called their wild call on the river, wolves devoured Pete's body. At the end of one more silent day a rider hallooed.

Getting no answer to his calls, Johnson rode into the open gateway through the low stockade, dismounted, entered the cabin, and saw how the place had been ransacked. Remounting, closing the gate on his still loaded pack horse, he was soon beside Pete's body at the top of the bluff. The skull was clearly Pete's—that of an old man with but one front tooth missing. The Bible was clearly Pete's, face down; Johnson picked it up, read for a moment the marked passage to which it was open, then thrust it into his jacket. Riding into the copse at last, he satisfied himself as to who had shot Pete.

Back by the cabin, he removed his supplies from his pack horse but left them in their tight bundles. He ate from such supplies as the young Assiniboine had left behind. Since his horses must rest after their long day's travel, he prepared now for sleep—cursing to see how much comfort Pete had made ready for his guests. But when he knocked out his pipe, Johnson took a blanket from a bunk and lay facing the door, on the floor. The door itself he left wide open.

Long before daylight, Johnson was back at the top of the bluff picking up Pete's scattered bones, for burial later with scalps. Next he packed just enough of his own supplies to last him a few days. He hid his rifle, of the same model as the Assiniboine's. By the time the red ball of the sun shone through the river's haze he was on the Assiniboine's trail.

Five horses had made a wide trail that any tenderfoot could have followed. Johnson contemptuously urged his mount to the gallop. Before long he had evidence that the confident Assiniboine had made his traveling days short and his camp stops long —rollicking along at the most leisurely pace, examining his prized loot. Johnson imagined how the Assiniboine must be contemplating himself as a man of wealth and prestige among his people. But his start of a day and a half would hardly be enough to keep him ahead of his pursuer. Spotting from a change of course that the warrior was headed for his tribe's big village, Johnson was the more determined that two days' pursuit must be enough.

The first night brought the winter's first piercing cold. The next day's ride was across a cold, crackling wilderness.

The second night the Assiniboine camped on the banks of a small stream. After freeing his unburdened horses to graze on the sparse vegetation and mosses along the bank, he took water from a hole knocked in the ice with his tomahawk and made a roaring driftwood fire. He had shot a goose that day, it seems. So along with Pete's coffee brewed in Pete's old coffeepot, and Pete's flour made into dough and browned on Pete's bread pan, he would have meat. He took time to build a second fire and to rake the first into a bed of live coals. He pulverized Pete's coffee beans with the blade of his tomahawk and set water to boiling. He spitted both legs of his goose. His hands were in biscuit dough when he heard a voice immediately by him.

"Kin I git invited fer supper?" Johnson asked him. The Liver-Eater stood warming his hands by the hospitable blaze of the new fire.

The Assiniboine had a moment's time to consider. His rifle, leaning against a tree, was nearer Johnson's reach than his own. His tomahawk lay ten feet away, by the rocks where he had pounded coffee beans. Though his knife was in his belt, he could not draw even this securely with his doughy hands.

"Kin' uv in a fix, red nigger?" Johnson said amiably. He gestured toward the water. "Jist step down ter ther crick an' wash yer han's."

The proud young Assiniboine snapped the dough from his hand and drew his knife. Johnson seized the knife arm and snapped it at the wrist, dealt him a great blow across the back of the neck, saved him from falling into the fire with a terrific kick that catapulted him over the coals, then sprang after him. The Assiniboine whirled and crouched to spring, but Johnson, still drawing no arms of his own, struck him across the face with a burning brand from the fire. As the blinded warrior staggered back, struggling to regain balance, his neck was broken by the smash of a fist to his jawbone. Johnson scalped him.

Johnson had saved the Assiniboine from falling into the fire, he explained later, to preserve his beautiful wolfskin jacket. Now he took the jacket, along with Pete's hooped scalp, and sat down to dinner. He had, he said, really cursed himself when he heard the honking of geese, for leaving his rifle behind. But he hadn't needed it, he found, after all.

Even as he ate, Johnson kept an eye to a storm building up around him. The Assiniboine, he thought, should have hurried on to his village with horses so laden, even if no avenger had been on his trail. Already, though his campfires were calm in the lee of a small cliff, great gusts of wind were howling across the prairies, and the first few giant snowflakes fell. Quickly rounding up all six horses, Johnson hobbled them out of the wind and not too far from the fires. Next he pulled some large logs from the banks of the creek, so that he could be assured of warmth. He gave each horse a share of Pete's shelled oats. One more move occurred to him while he sat smoking his pipe and drinking Pete's coffee: He must leave his trade-mark on the body of the dead Assiniboine.

Soon he had one last human liver in his hand. He hung it in a tree to windward of the fire, poked up the embers of the fire, and wrapped himself in his buffalo robe. He slept well.

By morning the wind had stopped, but the heavy snow was already six inches deep. Johnson reopened the hole in the ice, let the horses drink, gave them more oats, made up their packs, retrieved the frozen liver, and started back for Pete's cabin. He took his time on this return trip. On the morning of his fifth day out he saw Milk River, and soon Pete's bluff. He detoured into the copse of willows, now snowbound, in order to look the cabin over before showing himself. Peering over the brow of the hill, he saw smoke coming from the rock chimney and a strange horse feeding in the stockade. He cuddled the Assiniboine's rifle against his beard. At last a man came into sight, only to jump back at the sound of three sharp clicks—the cocking of the rifle. But Johnson was, as he always said of such an incident, ashamed not to have known his target sooner. Now he recognized Del Gue. He took his *remuda* into the enclosure; his mission was accomplished and he was home.

The long-time partners went on with Pete's trapping all that winter. His bones and scalp they buried on the bluff overlooking the river, then dug up again to rebury them by the Yellowstone, as on reflection they decided Pete would want. They had no further adventures that winter and saw almost no Indians. They did learn from a French-Canadian trapper that a party of Assiniboines had found the body of Johnson's victim and from its mutilated state realized the name of his killer.

Del asked no questions about the mutilation till after they had sold their furs and reburied Pete on the Yellowstone in the spring. But Del was never better off for not knowing what Johnson had done with a liver; he could always imagine most vividly. At last, twisting his huge set of whiskers, looking out over the Yellowstone where the partners had built a summer cabin, Del blurted out:

"Ye et thet Assiniboine's liver, didn't ye?"

"So ye fin'lly got 'roun' ter thet," Johnson said. "I see it war both'rin' ye but thort ye'd never ast."

"Whar's ther liver?" Del asked.

"Ye kain't keep livers in hot weather," Johnson said, and Del hoped the story would not be so lurid as to make him gag. "Ye 'member thet fine otter skin I helt out when we sol' our skins?" Johnson went on.

"Ther one hangin' hyar in ther cabin," Del said in acknowledgment.

"Thar's yer Injun liver," said the onetime Crow Killer.

Del opened his eyes in amazement. "Fust time I ever heerd o' baitin' a trap wi' Injun liver," he said, and went inside to look at the beautiful pelt. Johnson followed. "Almost like hevin' Pete back," Del said.

28 Lodge by the Sea

JOHNSON and Del trapped along the Yellowstone and then the Musselshell again through the middle and late 1880's. Always sharing their take equally, they made out surprisingly well. Del kept urging that they try Canada again, but after his one season in Alberta Johnson was resolved to stay in his own country. Nor would he move East for the fat offers made him by Buffalo Bill; Doc W. F. Carver, though he had originated such shows himself, laughed at the very idea of Liver-Eating Johnson leaving the West that was his.[1]

Well along in his sixties, Johnson was still huge, and still thought to be the most powerful man on the frontier. Beidler described him in 1887 as still of "magnificent physique" and fit "to take a hand with anyone . . . that wishes to collide with him." [2] Yet he must live now largely in the past. It was one of his special pleasures to visit the Crow Agency, often. There he was respected as a chief. More important, he could reminisce with his old enemies.

Del, though, still wanted better trapping; and though the two had been partners for most of their adult lives, they exchanged only the swift good-byes which the code of Mountain Men allowed them—Watch out for your scalp, and Might see you some

[1] The Carver mss., p. 69, suggest that Carver saw a chance to have a little fun with Cody by pushing him toward Johnson: "After I got back from my three-year trip to Europe and started the Wild West Show, Cody said to me one day, 'Doc, I believe I will try to get Liver-Eating Johnson.' I said, 'Do you know him?' He said he had seen him once and thought everybody would pay to see him. I said, 'Go ahead,' but . . . Bill wanted me to hunt him up. I kept after Bill for weeks to try to get Johnson, but when he saw he would have to make the proposition he cooled off. . . . Johnson would have done no more than throw him out through a closed door."

[2] Sanders, *History of Montana,* I, 233.

time, some place. Johnson stood by their cabin on the Yellow-stone and watched his old friend go.

In 1888 Johnson moved to Bear Creek. Building a cabin there, he went on trapping and hunting even after his unanimous election to be the first marshal at nearby Red Lodge.[3] Outlaws avoided Red Lodge now; and the occasional hassles with drunks, whom he handled with ease, left him plenty of time to get out to his traps or into the Big Snow Mountains for meat.

Johnson made good friends in Red Lodge. To the small boys he was an awesome being, about whom dreadful tales were told. He was somehow, at the same time, their friend. Ralph Lumley, sixty years later, remembered:

I was a small boy at the time he was town marshal here, and he was sure kind to the kids. . . . A road show would be put on in town. . . . The show hall as it was called had a large window in the back, and at that time money was scarce with children. There was a saloon adjoining the show hall and they used to throw out the empty beer barrels, and by placing a couple of these barrels alongside of the window we could see the show in progress.

One time four kids was standing on two barrels when we heard a booming voice say 'Get down off them barrels' and he pulled us down by the seats of the pants. I was in one of those seats. Two boys got away and we thought they were sure lucky not to have to go to jail. The marshal was a big man and he had on a bigger overcoat as it was winter. He took us to the front of the show, slapped his overcoat open and put it around us, one on each side, and walked right in without the ticket taker knowing what had been done. He sure liked the kids and sure had a kind heart toward them. The other boys were sorry they had run away.[4]

[3] "Red Lodge began in 1887 with the development of the Rocky Fork coal mines. The job of constable in a town of that size is not very excit-ing." Letter from Mrs. Anne McDonnell of the Historical Society of Montana to R. W. T., dated Helena, June 13, 1949.

[4] Ralph Lumley, letter to R. W. T., dated May 1, 1950, Red Lodge, Montana.

Red Lodge was only a small, new coal town. The citizens there, all Johnson's friends, knew that he was among them only because railroads and Jacob Haish's barbed wire had cut up the prairies and even straddled the mighty Rockies. The old forts and trading posts were tumbling. Outside of Red Lodge, men took for granted that Liver-Eating Johnson was dead. Took for granted? Why, they had heard the story of how he died: "Kilt, he war, in '70, I heerd; some Crows slipped up on him." And those who contradicted the stories of his death placed him variously: "Naw, Liver-Eatin' warn't kilt," an aged trapper insisted. "I seed a feller who camped wi' him on ther Chugwater, a few years ago."

Johnson may have taken to reminiscing a little in his last years. By contrast, for example, to Portuguese Phillips, who knew next to nothing of Johnson after hunting with him a number of times,[5] Pack-Saddle Ben Greenough knew a good deal about Johnson after their hunting and batching together one winter.[6] Johnson's neighbors knew he had been born in New Jersey.[7] He told George J. McDonald's father that he was of Scotch descent, not Irish, and that his name was really Johnston.[8] The people of Red Lodge gathered, at least, that many of his adventures had been along the Musselshell and that

> Brave, loyal and true, he
> Never shirked a duty,
> Never betrayed a friend—
> Never gave quarter to an enemy.[9]

[5] Phillips so told Doc Carver (Carver mss., p. 17).

[6] Letter from Ben Greenough to R. W. T. (Red Lodge, Montana, November 6, 1949), testifying, among other things, to Johnson's talking about White-Eye Anderson as an old companion.

[7] See *Carbon County Democrat,* February 7, 1900 (confirmation in letter to R. W. T. from F. J. Carey, Domiciliary Officer of the Veterans Administration in Los Angeles, June 23, 1949).

[8] George J. McDonald, letter to R. W. T., Red Lodge, June 15, 1949.

[9] Red Lodge *Picket,* February 16, 1900.

Johnson's health failed him all at once, around 1895. Though he was among kindly people who did everything possible for him as a matter of common hospitality and friendship, he fretted constantly about having to take charity. His last little plot of land had been sold by 1899. He had been one who prided himself on maintaining himself. Now he felt such pain at constantly taking that at last his friends felt he might be happier in the Old Soldiers' Home in Los Angeles. He must, surely, have felt some irony to be following Old John Hatcher, fifty years later, to the state Hatcher thought the proper place to die.

According to Veterans Administration records, "JOHNSTON, JOHN (also known as John Johnson)" entered the Veterans Hospital in December. One month later, to the day, on January 21, 1900, he died.

If Johnson could never live in a crowd, he was buried in one. To find the last resting place of the Crow Killer, the White Chief of the Shoshoni, the curious must drive from Los Angeles westward on Wilshire Boulevard, through Beverly Hills, past Westwood and the Country Club, and right on Sepulveda (a good name that: Big Anton's); half a mile along Sepulveda is the Cemetery gate.

Johnson's section of the Cemetery is "San Juan Hill." Here are tombstones marching in all directions, down into the little valleys and up over the little hills in what seem unending rows. There are no cairns here, such as Johnson helped build for Mad Mose or Bear Claw Chris Lapp, or such as his friends the Crows built for Crazy Woman. *Dapiek Absaroka* is in row "D," and the "tenderfoots" who walk past on their way to decorate other graves see no stakes round him, with grinning skulls. The second stone from the road (thar's no more trails) bears the abbreviated inscription,

JNO. JOHNSTON
CO. H
2ND COLO. CAV.